Parallel Learning Structures

Increasing Innovation in Bureaucracies

Gervase R. Bushe
Simon Fraser University

A. B. (Rami) Shani
California Polytechnic State University

ADDISON-WESLEY PUBLISHING COMPANY
Reading, Massachusetts • Menlo Park, California • New York
Don Mills, Ontario • Wokingham, England • Amsterdam • Bonn
Sydney • Singapore • Tokyo • Madrid • San Juan

Library of Congress Cataloging-in-Publication Data

Bushe, Gervase R.
    Parallel learning structures: increasing innovation in bureaucracies /
by Gervase R. Bushe & A.B. (Rami) Shani.
        p.   cm.
    Includes bibliographical references and index.
    ISBN 0-201-52427-9
    1. Organizational change.   2. Bureaucracy.   I. Shani,
Abraham B.   II. Title.
HD58.8.B885   1991
658.4'063—dc20   90-380
                                                           CIP

This book is in the Addison-Wesley Series on Organization Development.
Editors: Edgar H. Schein, Richard Beckhard

ABCDEFGHIJ–BA–943210

Other Titles in the Organization Development Series:

Managing in the New Team Environment:
Skills, Tools, and Methods
Larry Hirschhorn
1991 (52503)

This text is designed to help manage the tensions and complexities that arise for managers seeking to guide employees in a team environment. Based on an interactive video course developed at IBM, the text takes managers step by step through the process of building a team and authorizing it to act while they learn to step back and delegate. Specific issues addressed are how to give a team structure, how to facilitate its basic processes, and how to acknowledge differences in relationships among team members and between the manager and individual team members.

The Strategic Management Process: Integrating the OD
Perspective
David Hitchin and Walter Ross
1991 (52429)

Written for CEOs, general managers, OD professionals, and strategic-planning specialists, this text integrates the OD perspective into the strategic-management process. This approach begins with the authors' belief that building and sustaining a healthy, high-performance organization is dependent upon the fact that people are the key to organizational success, and that their management is critical to successful strategic planning and execution. The authors' philosophy and suggestions for the strategic management of both profit and nonprofit organizations are presented.

The Conflict-Positive Organization: Stimulate Diversity and
Create Unity
Dean Tjosvold
1991 (51485)

This book describes how managers and employees can use conflict to find common ground, solve problems, and strengthen morale and relationships. By showing how well-managed conflict invigorates and empowers teams and organizations, the text demonstrates how conflict is vital for a company's continuous improvement and increased competitive advantage.

Change by Design
Robert R. Blake, Jane Srygley Mouton, and Anne Adams McCanse
1989 (50748)

This book develops a systematic approach to organization development and provides readers with rich illustrations of coherent planned change. The book involves testing, examining, revising, and strengthening conceptual foundations in order to create sharper corporate focus and increased predictability of successful organization development.

Organization Development in Health Care
R. Wayne Boss
1989 (18364)
This is the first book to discuss the intricacies of the health care industry. The book explains the impact of OD in creating healthy and viable organizations in the health care sector. Through unique and innovative techniques, hospitals are able to reduce nursing turnover, thereby resolving the nursing shortage problem. The text also addresses how OD can improve such bottom-line variables as cash flow and net profits.

Self-Designing Organizations: Learning How to Create High Performance
Susan Albers Mohrman and Thomas G. Cummings
1989 (14603)
This book looks beyond traditional approaches to organizational transition, offering a strategy for developing organizations that enables them to learn not only how to adjust to the dynamic environment in which they exist, but also how to achieve a higher level of performance. This strategy assumes that change is a learning process: the goal is continually refined as organizational members learn how to function more effectively and respond to dynamic conditions in their environment.

Power and Organization Development: Mobilizing Power to Implement Change
Larry E. Greiner and Virginia E. Schein
1988 (12185)
This book forges an important collaborative approach between two opposing and often contradictory approaches to management: OD practitioners who espouse a "more humane" workplace without understanding the political realities of getting things done, and practicing managers who feel comfortable with power but overlook the role of human potential in contributing to positive results.

Designing Organizations for High Performance
David P. Hanna
1988 (12693)
This book is the first to give insight into the actual processes you can use to translate organizational concepts into bottom-line improvements. Hanna's "how-to" approach shows not only the successful methods of intervention, but also the plans behind them and the corresponding results.

Process Consultation, Volume 1: Its Role in Organization Development, Second Edition
Edgar H. Schein
1988 (06736)

How can a situation be influenced in the workplace without the direct use of power or formal authority? This book presents the core theoretical foundations and basic prescriptions for effective management.

Organizational Transitions: Managing Complex Change, Second Edition
Richard Beckhard and Reuben T. Harris
1987 (10887)
This book discusses the choices involved in developing a management system appropriate to the "transition state." It also discusses commitment to change, organizational culture, and increasing and maintaining productivity, creativity, and innovation.

Organization Development: A Normative View
W. Warner Burke
1987 (10697)
This book concisely describes and defines the theories and practices of organization development and also looks at organization development as change in an organization's culture. It is a useful guide to the field of organization development and is invaluable to managers, executives, practitioners, and anyone desiring an excellent overview of this multifaceted field.

Team Building: Issues and Alternatives, Second Edition
William G. Dyer
1987 (18037)
Through the use of the techniques and procedures described in this book, managers and consultants can effectively prepare, apply, and follow up on the human processes affecting the productive functioning of teams.

The Technology Connection: Strategy and Change in the Information Age
Marc S. Gerstein
1987 (12188)
This is a book that guides managers and consultants through crucial decisions about the use of technology for increasing effectiveness and competitive advantage. It provides a useful way to think about the relationship between information technology, business strategy, and the process of change in organizations.

Stream Analysis: A Powerful Way to Diagnose and Manage Organizational Change
Jerry I. Porras
1987 (05693)
Drawing on a conceptual framework that helps the reader to better understand organizations, this book shows how to diagnose failings in organizational functioning and how to plan a comprehensive set of actions needed to change the organization into a more effective system.

Process Consultation, Volume II: Lessons for Managers and Consultants
Edgar H. Schein

1987 (06744)

This book shows the viability of the process consultation model for working with human systems. Like Schein's first volume on process consultation, the second volume focuses on the moment-to-moment behavior of the manager or consultant rather than on the design of the OD program.

Managing Conflict: Interpersonal Dialogue and Third-Party Roles, Second Edition
Richard E. Walton

1987 (08859)

This book shows how to implement a dialogue approach to conflict management. It presents a framework for diagnosing recurring conflicts and suggests several basic options for controlling or resolving them.

Pay and Organization Development
Edward E. Lawler

1981 (03990)

This book examines the important role that reward systems play in organization development efforts. By combining examples and specific recommendations with conceptual material, it organizes the various topics and puts them into a total systems perspective. Specific pay approaches such as gainsharing, skill-based pay, and flexible benefits are discussed and their impact on productivity and the quality of work life is analyzed.

Work Redesign
J. Richard Hackman and Greg R. Oldham

1980 (02779)

This book is a comprehensive, clearly written study of work design as a strategy for personal and organizational change. Linking theory and practical technologies, it develops traditional and alternative approaches to work design that can benefit both individuals and organizations.

Organizational Dynamics: Diagnosis and Intervention
John P. Kotter

1978 (03890)

This book offers managers and OD specialists a powerful method of diagnosing organizational problems and of deciding when, where, and how to use (or not use) the diverse and growing number of organizational improvement tools that are available today. Comprehensive and fully integrated, the book includes many different concepts, research findings, and competing philosophies and provides specific examples of how to use the information to improve organizational functioning.

Career Dynamics: Matching Individual and Organizational Needs
Edgar H. Schein

1978 (06834)

This book studies the complexities of career development from both an individual and an organizational perspective. Changing needs throughout the adult life cycle, interaction of work and family, and integration of individual and organizational goals through human resource planning and development are all thoroughly explored.

Matrix
Stanley M. Davis and Paul Lawrence

1977 (01115)

This book defines and describes the matrix organization, a significant departure from the traditional "one man-one boss" management system. The author notes that the tension between the need for independence (fostering innovation) and order (fostering efficiency) drives organizations to consider a matrix system. Among the issues addressed are reasons for using a matrix, methods for establishing one, the impact of the system on individuals, its hazards, and what types of organizations can use a matrix system.

Feedback and Organization Development: Using Data-Based Methods
David A. Nadler

1977 (05006)

This book addresses the use of data as a tool for organizational change. It attempts to bring together some of what is known from experience and research and to translate that knowledge into useful insights for those who are thinking about using data-based methods in organizations. The broad approach of the text is to treat a whole range of questions and issues considering the various uses of data as an organizational change tool.

Designing Complex Organizations
Jay Galbraith

1973 (02559)

This book attempts to present an analytical framework of the design of organizations, particularly of types of organizations that apply lateral decision processes or matrix forms. These forms have become pervasive in all types of organizations, yet there is little systematic public knowledge about them. This book helps fill this gap.

Organization Development: Strategies and Models
Richard Beckhard

1969 (00448)

This book is written for managers, specialists, and students of management who are concerned with the planning of organization development programs to resolve the dilemmas brought about by a rapidly changing environment. Practiced teams of interdependent people must spend real time improving their methods of working, decision making, and communicating, and a planned, managed change is the first step toward effecting and maintaining these improvements.

Organization Development: Its Nature, Origins, and Prospects
Warren G. Bennis

1969 (00523)

This primer on OD is written with an eye toward the people in organizations who are interested in learning more about this educational strategy as well as for those practitioners and students of OD who may want a basic statement both to learn from and to argue with. The author treats the subject with a minimum of academic jargon and a maximum of concrete examples drawn from his own and others' experience.

Developing Organizations: Diagnosis and Action
Paul R. Lawrence and Jay W. Lorsch

1969 (04204)

This book is a personal statement of the authors' evolving experience, through research and consulting, in the work of developing organizations. The text presents the authors' overview of organization development, then proceeds to examine issues at each of three critical interfaces: the organization-environment interface, the group-group interface, and the individual-organization interface, including brief examples of work on each. The text concludes by pulling the themes together in a set of conclusions about organizational development issues as they present themselves to practicing managers.

About the Authors

Gervase R. Bushe (Ph.D., Case Western Reserve University) is Associate Professor of Organizational Behavior in the Faculty of Business Administration at Simon Fraser University, in the Vancouver suburb of Burnaby, British Columbia. He is also a senior partner in the consulting firm Discovery & Design and director of professional development for Northwest Human Systems Development Practitioners. He has had experience as an internal and external OD consultant and his work has covered many different facets of the field, including team building, action research, union-management, quality of work life, organizational design, quality control, organizational culture, and executive group process. He has a special interest in change agents and change agentry and has been a teacher of change agents for over ten years.

   A. B. (Rami) Shani (Ph.D., Case Western Reserve University) is a Professor of Organization Behavior and Management in the School of Business at California Polytechnic State University. As an action researcher, he has worked with diverse organizations and industries in different countries. He has published articles dealing with sociotechnical systems design, action research methodology, organizational design, and parallel learning structures in a variety of journals. He is the co-author (with Jim Lau) of *Behavior in Organizations*. Rami is currently active in action research projects that attempt to foster innovation through optimizing interfaces between technology management, strategy, and organizational design.

Foreword

The Addison-Wesley Series on Organization Development originated in the late 1960s when a number of us recognized that the rapidly growing field of "OD" was not well understood or well defined. We also recognized that there was no one OD philosophy, and hence one could not at that time write a textbook on the theory and practice of OD, but one could make clear what various practitioners were doing under that label. So the original six books launched what has since become a continuing enterprise, the essence of which was to allow different authors to speak for themselves instead of trying to summarize under one umbrella what was obviously a rapidly growing and highly diverse field.

By the early 1980s the series included nineteen titles. OD was growing by leaps and bounds, and it was expanding into all kinds of organizational areas and technologies of intervention. By this time, many textbooks existed as well that tried to capture the core concepts of the field, but we felt that diversity and innovation were still the more salient aspects of OD.

Now as we move into the 1990s our series includes twenty-seven titles, and we are beginning to see some real convergence in the underlying assumptions of OD. As we observe how different professionals working in different kinds of organizations and occupational communities make their case, we see we are still far from having a single "theory" of organization development. Yet, a set of common assumptions is surfacing. We are beginning to see patterns in what works and what does not work, and we are becoming more articulate about these patterns. We are also seeing the field connecting to broader themes in the organizational sciences, and new theories and theories of practice are being presented in such areas as conflict resolution, group dynamics, and the process of change in relationship to culture. The new titles in the series address current themes directly: Tjosvold's *The Conflict-Positive Organization,* for example, connects to a whole research tradition on the dynamics of collaboration, competition, and conflict; Hirschhorn's *Managing in the New Team Environment* contains important links to psychoanalytic group theory; Bushe and Shani's *Parallel Learning Structures* presents a seminal theory of large-scale organization change based on the institution of parallel systems as change agents; and Hitchin and Ross's *The Strategic Management Process* looks at the connection between strategic planning theory and practice and implementation through OD interventions.

As editors we have not dictated these connections, nor have we asked authors to work on higher order concepts and theories. It is just happening, and it is a welcome turn of events. Perhaps it is an indication that OD may be reaching a period of consolidation and integration. We hope that we can contribute to this trend with future volumes.

Cambridge, Massachusetts Richard H. Beckhard
New York, New York Edgar H. Schein

Preface

There is some evidence that the field of organization development (OD) emerged as a response to the excesses and failures of bureaucracy.[1] In the late 1960s and early '70s some leading OD scholars predicted the imminent collapse of bureaucratic organization.[2] Yet, as we move into the 1990s bureaucracies are still going strong. OD oriented managers and consultants tend to be at odds with bureaucracies: We don't like them, and we don't really know how to handle them. Though OD has always been defined as a system-wide change effort, we believe that a relatively small percentage of OD consultants have ever been involved in a large system change project.[3] Most often, a consultant works with a department or subunit of the organization. In bureaucratic systems they find themselves running into walls created by the very design of the organization. A few can recognize this and work with it. Most, however, attribute their lack of success either to "the system"—that mysterious, recalcitrant, and overwhelming destroyer of good ideas and intentions—or to bad management.

From our point of view, an understanding of organization design is absolutely essential for any large-scale organizational change effort. When there are too many people involved to get them

---

1. For examples, see Beckhard (1969), Friedlander and Brown (1974).

2. For example, Bennis (1966).

3. Cf. Mohrman, Mohrman, Ledford, Cummings, and Lawler (1989).

all in a room to make a decision, we need other interventions. From what we can see, the 1990s will be a decade of extensive experimentation with new organization designs for driving developmental processes and achieving many of the ends of conventional OD: more humanized, empowering, effective, productive, and nourishing work organizations. This is not a book on organizational design, but there are many good ones that should be available to anyone managing large systems change.[4]

This is a book on a technostructural intervention that promotes system-wide change in bureaucracies, while retaining the advantages of bureaucratic design. "Parallel learning structures" are an intervention that managers and consultants have implicitly used to implement system-wide changes. Yet little has been written on them, and much of it contradictory, so managers and consultants still have no resource to help them think through the issues associated with the intervention.[5]

That's what this book is—a resource of models and theories built around five cases of parallel learning structures that can help those who create and maintain them be more effective and successful. For those of you who like to skip around in books, here's a quick outline. Chapter 1 defines technostructural interventions, discusses the advantages and disadvantages of bureaucracy, and briefly defines parallel learning structures. The next five chapters describe cases in diverse organizations and industries. Each case focuses on a different use for a parallel structure. At the end of each case we discuss techniques and theoretical issues that come up in almost all parallel structure interventions. If you are not interested in every case, you may want to skim the theory sections. Chapter 7 provides a general map for implementing a parallel learning structure, and Chapter 8 offers a series of lenses to help you understand the processes of learning and change associated with this technostructural intervention.

---

4. Each of the following provides a useful and different perspective: Miller and Rice (1967), Galbraith (1977), Tichy (1983), Mintzberg (1983), Lawrence and Dyer (1983), Miller and Friesen (1984), MacKenzie (1986), Nadler and Tushman (1988), Pasmore (1988), Kilmann (1989).

5. For a review of the literature on parallel structures, see Bushe and Shani (1990).

For those who are already working with parallel structures, we hope the book stimulates your thinking and sharpens your interventions. For those who are new to parallel learning structures, we hope it provides enough practical advice to help you decide when and how to use them. And for OD scholars, we hope the book stimulates more research on the functioning and outcomes of parallel learning structures.

ACKNOWLEDGMENTS

Many, many people have contributed to the development of our thinking about parallel learning structures over the past ten years. As graduate students in the department of organizational behavior at Case Western Reserve University in the late 1970s and early 1980s we were surrounded by people involved in large system change projects at major corporations. It was in the informal discussions and sharing of experiences with fellow doctoral students like Marty Kaplan, Gene Bocialetti, Mike McCarthy, and Dick Cogan that we first noticed a common thread that we later came to define as the parallel learning structure. All the members of the faculty were important sources of intellectual stimulation. Dave Kolb, Ron Fry, Don Wolfe, Eric Neilsen, and Suresh Srivastva shaped our understanding of learning in organizations. Dave Brown, Frank Friedlander, Bob Kaplan, and Bill Pasmore gave us an appreciation of the technostructural dynamics in organizational change processes. Bill, in particular, has been an ongoing source of professional support for both of us.

Since graduating from Case, there have been many other colleagues and clients who have enriched our thinking. Gervase would like to acknowledge the contributions that Tom Pitman, Howard Carlson, Kathy MacDonald, Drew Danko, and Larry Szeliga have made to his understanding of parallel learning structures and to the quality of his life in general. Rami would like to acknowledge the collegial excitement, challenge, and support that Ord Elliott, Tom Basuray, Bruce Eberhardt, and Mike Stebbins have provided to his ongoing learning about parallel structure phenomena.

We'd also like to acknowledge each other. This book really was a synergistic effort with equal contribution to the final product and could not have been completed without a combination of our experiences and energy.

And, finally, we must acknowledge our wives, Vera and Elaine, who have put up with the neglect that a writing project like this creates and who have always been there when it really counted

Vancouver, British Columbia G.R.B
San Luis Obispo, California A.B.S

Contents

1

Introduction

A nonunionized semiconductor manufacturer wants to increase the amount of innovation in, and overall effectiveness of, its operations. It creates a structure for employees to propose ideas, gather resources, meet in small groups on company time, and support implementation of new ideas that gather support.

A bank decides to improve its responsiveness to the environment and its ability to take advantage of opportunities. It creates a structure for employees to propose areas in need of attention, generate small groups to work on these areas, and implement solutions that emerge.

A unionized automotive manufacturer tries to improve its adaptability, its effectiveness, and the quality of work life. In partnership with the local union, it creates a structure for employees to meet regularly to identify and solve problems, gather necessary resources to solve those problems, and increase cooperation between all levels of the plant.

A hospital wants to explore alternative ways of providing service. It creates a structure for employees to propose ideas, meet in small groups to further refine those ideas, and provide support and resources for implementing those ideas.

A Department of Education in a university wishes to improve the quality of education in a county school system with fifteen districts. A structure is created that integrates the various school districts, state bodies, and universities as a vehicle for comprehensive educational reform.

A manufacturing organization attempts to implement new quality control technologies. The techniques are quite simple, but their use directly violates a number of political and cultural norms within the organization. They create a structure of overlapping groups from the plant manager on down to the shop floor. The senior management steering committee sanctions groups that want to try applying these new techniques and ensures that the groups have the resources and support they need. As they learn from their success and failures, changes in the basic design of the organization are made to help institutionalize the use of these quality techniques.

Each of these vignettes briefly describes the use of a technostructural intervention to aid a bureaucratic organization in becoming more innovative and adaptable and/or to attain some complex organizational purpose. We call these interventions "parallel learning structures." They are one of the most important innovations in organizational development (OD) technology developed during the 1980s. In this book we will look at the theory and practice of parallel learning structure interventions in different types of bureaucratic organization. To begin with, let's briefly look at what we mean by the term "technostructural intervention."

Technostructural Intervention

A technostructural intervention is a change in the technology and/or structure of an organization with the purpose of improving or stabilizing the entire sociotechnical system in that organization. "Sociotechnical system" is a term coined at the Tavistock Institute in England to highlight the fact that all organizations are composed of a technical system (the technology, formal structure, rules and regulations) and a social system (informal groups, cliques, patterns of interaction) nested in an environment. Historically, most OD work has focused on the social system. In the past decade, more attention has been paid to both the technical system and the environment. Sociotechnical systems theory[1] has been the guiding force in such technostructural innovations as autonomous workgroups and

---

1. C. Trist (1981), Pasmore (1988). For a brief synopsis, see Appendix A.

technical design based on variance analysis. Work redesign is another example of a widely used technostructural intervention. Quality circles are a more recent technostructural intervention being used by some OD practitioners.

Some of the early theory that greatly influenced OD focused on technostructural issues. Chris Argyris's early work showed how the structure of bureaucratic organizations was in conflict with adult development. Rensis Likert's System 4 involved the use of a specific type of organizing structure. The matrix form of organizational structure emerged out of pioneering OD work in the aerospace and electronics industries.

A technostructural intervention could be the primary intervention or a supporting intervention in a planned change process. Like any change process, it can be used for first-order change (i.e., a change that helps to maintain the basic character of the system, like a tune-up) or second-order change (i.e., a change that affects the fundamental character of the system, like putting jet engines in a car). Some people view structural change with suspicion. These are people who have lived through one or more "reorganizations" where a lot of time and energy was spent but "nothing really changed." In these cases, we are probably dealing with a first-order change—the boxes on the organization chart were moved around, but the underlying logic of the boxes remained the same. A technostructural intervention will not result in second-order change unless there is a real change in the basic elements of structure, and even then, there are no guarantees.

Structure is the division and coordination of labor. Organizations exist because there is something to do that requires more than one person; therefore, the work is divided up among several employees. Once the work is divided up, some way has to be found to coordinate the efforts of these individuals to ensure that the final product or service comes together. Structures are environments that affect how people behave. They channel effort and energy in a particular direction. When they are well designed, they support employees in accomplishing their tasks; when they are poorly designed, they can get in the way. Since they channel effort, changes in structure can lead to changes in how people behave at work.

Take, for example, the number of employees a person has to supervise. Direct supervision is one way of coordinating employees. The number of employees a person supervises is a result of the division of labor. Imagine a person who has three people to supervise, and little else to do. We are likely to find that this person is constantly peering over the shoulder of his or her subordinates, getting involved in all their decisions, and rarely calling group meetings, preferring instead to deal with each one individually. In fact, we would probably find that this supervisor behaves like McGregor's "theory X" manager.[2] We might attribute this behavior to the manager's personality, attitudes, or values. Give the same supervisor forty people to supervise, and we're likely to find that he or she is now delegating decision making, permitting subordinates to make their own choices, using group meetings for departmental coordination, and, in general, acting more like a "theory Y" manager. In our experience, people tend to attribute poor supervision to personality flaws, warped values, and/or lack of training, but we often find that poor supervision is a result of poor structure. There is something in the organization that makes it seem to be in a person's best interest to act in a less than optimal way. No amount of training, process consultation, or therapy is going to change anything while the structure stays the same. Therefore, we think of technostructural interventions as attempts to sculpt environments to support a particular set of behaviors.

One of the causes of OD failure is the attempt to develop a new set of behaviors within a structure that supported old behaviors. Sometimes this can get ridiculous. Take, for example, the attempt to increase worker participation in factories through training managers in participative management. The vast majority of factories coordinate worker labor through the standardization of work processes. In practice, this means that the actual work people do is designed by engineers in some corporate office who have little contact with either the workers or their supervisors. Each task is designed to fit with all the others. Few people outside of the engineering staff will actually understand how all the various operations fit together. What coordinates people's labor is the work itself, the standardization built into the design. But what decisions are these workers going to participate in when neither they nor their supervisors have any say over their work and don't really know how their part fits into the whole? Discussions about fairly minor matters, such as housekeeping, parking lots, tool cribs, and machine maintenance

---

2. McGregor (1960).

are possible, but they wear thin after a year or two. In the long run, real employee involvement in decision making in factories requires change in the way the typical factory is structured.

More than other types of OD interventions, structural interventions have to be actively supported by the top of the organization. Over a decade ago Barry Oshry pointed out what many current writers on "transformational leadership" are now saying, that the basic ways in which those at the top influence an organization are through (a) providing compelling visions that capture employee energy and commitment, and (b) providing structures that channel that energy toward that vision.[3] In most cases, a structural intervention is going to affect everyone in the organization and will have to be sanctioned by the person who sits at the very top of the organization. Therefore, technostructural interventions are strategic interventions. They require a vision of what the change is about, expounded by senior management. They are not the sort of thing that a manager or OD consultant can pull out of his or her pocket in a pinch. They generally require a lot of up-front planning with senior management, a fairly long-term perspective, and trained internal resource people to aid in implementation.

Parallel learning structures are used in bureaucratic organizations. Before moving on, it would probably be useful to describe what we mean by bureaucracy and why bureaucracies need parallel learning structures.

What Is Bureaucracy and Why Does It Persist?

All organizations, however designed, share certain attributes. All involve a division and coordination of tasks; all transform inputs into outputs; all involve information processing; and all require an uneven distribution of legitimate authority. The essence of bureaucratic organization is the production of standardized, predictable, replicable performance by many different people and/or groups. It is bureaucracy that makes every Big Mac the same, that ensures that a federal tax return filed in Chicago is assessed the same way as one filed in Miami, and that allows you to pick up a phone, dial a few digits, and call any other phone in North America within seconds.

---

3. Oshry, B. (1977).

And, in the case of mass production, bureaucracy results in the lowest costs. How many people could afford hand-crafted automobiles, stoves, washing machines, televisions, and the plethora of consumer goods we've all come to expect? Amazing as it may seem to those who equate bureaucracy with mountains of red tape and nonresponsiveness, efficiency (the most output for the least input) is the hallmark of the bureaucratic organization. So how do bureaucracies do this? Some of the basic parameters are centralized control, task specialization, functional grouping, and internal standardization.

Centralized Control. The fewer the number of people who decide what the organization will do (define its ends) or how to do it (define its means), the more centralized the control. Of course, centralization is a relative term. The larger the organization, the more people will be involved in decisions, though the actual ratio of decision makers to non–decision makers may decrease. The more centralized the control, the more focused the organization. In addition, centralized control greatly increases the standardization of outcomes—for example, a very small number of people decide how a very large number of people will cook Big Macs. It also reduces the time and expense that would be involved if every separate unit had to decide on means or ends for itself—for example, insurance agents at different branches don't have to spend time analyzing what their rates or packages should be. Thus centralized control leads to replicable performance and to certain efficiencies.

Task Specialization and Accountability. In a bureaucracy, every individual has a specific job for which he or she is accountable. The further down in the hierarchy, the more specialized the job. Bureaucracies divide large, complex tasks (e.g., manufacturing and selling TVs) into many small, simple jobs. This greatly reduces the training time and expense needed to enable people to make a productive contribution to the organization. As individuals specialize in a particular task, their skill at performing that task tends to increase, leading to more reliable, replicable performance.

Functional Grouping. Organizations group people together into units for coordination. In bureaucracies, people are almost always grouped by function; that is, the task or specialty they perform for the organization. This leads to an economy of scale as specialists can be used part-time by other units. Instead of having one industrial engineer for each assembly line, a pool of six industrial engineers looks after ten assembly lines. Employees do not lose valuable time in migrating from one job to another. Also, time is not lost changing locations and tools, because people typically have only one job at one place. And by belonging to a group of other like specialists, innovations in their specialty are more likely to get diffused among them.

Internal Standardization. In addition to functional grouping, bureaucracies coordinate work through rules, regulations, and standardization of work processes and/or skills. By designing how each individual task should be done and then ensuring that people do it that way, standardization of work processes builds coordination of work right into the job design. Rules and regulations provide a similar coordinating device. In both cases, people do not need to meet together to coordinate their work, and face-to-face coordination is the most expensive kind. Standardization of skills refers to the practice of buying highly skilled talent and then operating on the assumption that prior training has instilled a set of work procedures and values the organization can count on. Bureaucracies like hospitals, universities, and accounting firms all depend to some extent on standardization of skills. If an organization relies primarily on personal interaction for coordination of work, it is not a bureaucracy.

Problems of Learning and Adaptation

Any strength taken to excess becomes a weakness, and there are certainly cases of organizations becoming too centralized, specialized, and standardized. But even when a bureaucracy has a healthy dose of these attributes, it still is going to have problems *learning and adapting,* because each attribute that helps ensure predictable, replicable performance gets in the way of learning, adaptation, and change.

Centralized Control. If people work at the boundaries of an organization and are constantly interacting with the organization's environment, they have important information that's needed for organizational adaptation. Under centralized control, however, that information is probably not going to be heard or acted on. Similarly, the people who actually do the work or provide the service of the organization probably know a lot about how that work could be optimized. By controlling people's actions from some centralized "head"quarters, there is less possibility that people will adapt to deal with local conditions. If individuals aren't adapting, the organization isn't adapting.

Task Specialization. Task specialization narrowly focuses people on one small aspect of the overall organization. As a result, they often don't understand the "big picture" and can do little to help the organization adapt and improve itself. Furthermore, task specialization makes individuals less adaptable as they know how to do only a few things.

Functional Grouping. Functional grouping tends to break an organization up into differentiated subcultures with different goals, values, and beliefs. Functions may even have competing or conflicting goals, which builds conflict right into the structure of the organization. Intergroup competition and conflict make it difficult for the organization to gather and process information required for learning across boundaries. It also makes it very difficult to implement large-scale changes across these boundaries.

Internal Standardization. Rules and standards are the results of past acts of organizational learning.[4] When they are successful, they become very hard to change, even when there are new and better routines available. Like centralized control, the use of rules and standards reduces the likelihood that individuals will be able to adapt to local conditions.

A "Simple" Solution

The attributes of bureaucratic design just presented don't come close to capturing all the barriers to learning in organizations, and we will discuss barriers to learning in more detail in Chapter 8. We wanted to focus on some of the structural aspects of the problem because we, in the OD field, tend to underemphasize or ignore structure. By paying attention to these design attributes we discover a fundamen-

---

4. Levitt and March (1988).

tal paradox; that it is those attributes that lead to high, predictable performance that get in the way of the learning needed to adapt and sustain high, predictable performance. The complicated answer is to try and totally redesign the bureaucratic organization into one that is good at both efficiency and learning. The "simple" answer is to build a second structure that is designed for learning that supplements, but doesn't replace, the bureaucracy. This book is about this second option. It is about designing structures that do not have much in the way of centralized control, task specialization, functional grouping, or internal standardization. In fact, it is about building supplemental structures that have exactly the opposite attributes.

Defining Parallel Learning Structures

One of the reasons that parallel learning structure interventions are not widely discussed in OD textbooks at this time is that they have been given so many different names.[5] Problems of interpretation have been compounded because sometimes the same name is used to describe very different interventions and other times different names are used to label the same thing. We are not too concerned about the name, and we don't believe there is any one best way to structure the intervention. We offer the term "parallel learning structure" as a generic label to cover interventions where: (a) a "structure" (that is, a specific division and coordination of labor) is created that (b) operates "parallel" (that is, in tandem or side-by-side) with the formal hierarchy and structure and (c) has the purpose of increasing an organization's "learning" (that is, the creation and/or implementation of new thoughts and behaviors by employees).

---

5. For example, *collateral organization* (Zand, 1974, 1981; Nadler, 1977; Susman, 1981; Kilmann, 1982; Rubinstein and Woodman, 1984), *parallel organization* (Carlson in Miller, 1978; Stein and Kanter, 1980; Bushe, Danko, and Long, 1984; Moore, 1986; Moore and Miners, 1988), *parallel structures* (Shani and Bushe, 1987), *dualistic structures* (Goldstein, 1978, 1985), *shadow structures* (Schein and Greiner, 1977), *action research systems* (Shani and Pasmore, 1985), *circular organizations* (Ackoff, 1981), *parallel learning structures* (Bushe and Shani, 1990), and *vertical linking* (Hawley, 1984). In addition, a number of reports of change projects implicitly describe the use of such supplemental structures without labeling them (e.g., Brekelmans and Jonsson, 1976; Emery and Thorsrud, 1976; Drexler and Lawler, 1977; Adizes, 1979; Pasmore and Friedlander, 1982; Greenbaum, Holden, and Spataro, 1983; Shea, 1986).

We have also found that the term "parallel structure" is the one that seems to stay with people most easily and evokes a fairly accurate image of the intervention. Throughout the book we'll use the terms "parallel learning structure" and "parallel structure" interchangeably.

We will describe parallel learning structures in greater detail throughout the book. At this point, let's just note that in its most basic form, a parallel learning structure consists of a steering committee that provides overall direction and authority and a number of small groups with norms and operating procedures that promote a climate conducive to innovation, learning, and group problem solving. Members of the parallel learning structure are also members of the formal organization, though within the parallel learning structure their relationships are not limited by the formal chain of command. Some parallel learning structures are set up on a temporary basis, while others are intended to be permanent.

The key thing about parallel structures is that they create a bounded space and time for thinking, talking, deciding, and acting differently than normally takes place at work. If you don't implement different norms and procedures, you don't have a parallel structure. The most important and difficult task for the people creating the parallel learning structure is to create a different culture within it.

It isn't the supplemental structure that's important. What's important is that people act in a way that promotes learning and adaptation. Most of us are not so evolved that we can operate in ambiguity and flexibly change styles to fit the occasion. This is the Achilles' heel of many of the new organizational designs that create loose roles and ambiguous responsibilities. Some people thrive in loosely structured organizations, but most don't. The designs that work in the long run, without regressing to more authoritarian forms, seem to have much clearer role definitions and procedures—they pay attention to the content of people's jobs as well as the process. People operating in tightly designed bureaucracies cannot be expected to know how and when it is appropriate to follow procedures and when to question them. So to reduce ambiguity and confusion, bureaucracies discourage deviance. The problem is that in systems where procedures are never questioned, mangers develop an oversimplified, insular, distorted and, eventually, self-destructive view of their organization. Questioning, puzzlement, and doubt are needed for learning and adaptation to take place.

The parallel learning structure provides a time and place where organizational inquiry is legitimate. Its existence tells people this is where it is okay to question, to express doubts and reservations. When you're in the parallel structure, your role is to question the organization and promote change. When you're in the formal organization, your role is to comply with the organization and maintain its stability. This simple bounding of time, space, and role increases the possibility that some people might actually summon the courage to speak up and say the unsayable, question the unquestionable, and bring to light what the system has been trying so hard to not see. Of course, simply setting up a parallel structure will not, in and of itself, make people more courageous. But establishing clear boundaries and role expectations that build legitimacy for such behaviors surely increases the possibility that people will risk a different way of behaving at work.

To further clarify what we are dealing with in this book, the following are *not* parallel learning structure interventions:

> *Task Forces and Teams.* The key feature distinguishing parallel learning structures from a set of task forces is the emphasis on creating the kinds of norms and procedures that facilitate learning and innovation. Unless specific interventions are made, task forces mirror the norms and procedures of the formal organization. In addition, task forces tend to be set up by a manager. Parallel learning structures always involve a steering committee.
>
> *Matrix and Project-Management Structures.* Parallel learning structures do not have dual authority or reporting relations and the composition of groups is not based solely on functional expertise.
>
> *Semiautonomous Work Teams.* This is a way to design the formal organization of manufacturing. Such teams do not operate in parallel, and are mainly concerned with producing goods (not learning).
>
> *Industrial Democracy.* Joint determination generally involves setting up some form of works council, but these are oriented more toward defining organizational policy than

generating innovation. In addition, norms and procedures tend to be highly formalized and oriented more toward maintaining order and equity than supporting group problem solving.

Plan for the Book

This book is about the use of parallel learning structure interventions in organizations that are particularly poor at learning: bureaucracies. Bureaucratic organizations are those that coordinate the activities of their employees through standardization and rules. They exist because they are the most successful way we know of organizing when tasks can be programmed and routinized.

In Chapters 2–6, we look at cases of different applications of parallel learning structures for different ends. In each of these chapters, we will look at cases where parallel learning structures have had very different purposes and comment on the theory and practice of using alternative structures to accomplish each purpose. At the end of each case, we comment on the important theoretical issues in the case that help to guide action. In each case, the name of the organization has been changed.

In some sense, each case is about different aspects of generating learning in organizations. In Chapter 2, we look at the issue of designing organizations for simultaneous efficiency and innovation and describe why some of the newer attempts to do that don't work. We look at the promise of parallel learning structures for adding an adaptive capacity to organizations that are designed for efficiency. In Chapter 3, we look at the problems of developing learning in highly fragmented and politicized systems and some of the opportunities parallel structures create for overcoming them. In Chapter 3, we also look at the process of learning within the parallel structure (action research) and some of the emergent qualities of that process that consultants must manage. Chapter 4 confronts us with the problems of diffusing learning when it calls for radical change in patterns of work. Here we look at the parallel structure's ability to provide a vehicle for incremental learning about a transformational change and the role of experts in that process. Chapter 5 returns us to issues of politics and fragmentation. Here we focus on the potential of the parallel structure for organizational integration and the transformation of destructive power dynamics into constructive ones. Finally, in Chapter 6, we explore the possibility of the parallel structure being a precursor to total redesign of the organization by teaching people about new ways of organizing before they redesign their current organization. While each theory section is specifically tied to the focus of the chapter, each has something to say about every parallel learning structure intervention.

In Chapter 7, we bring together all the different experiences with parallel structures to develop a general, step-by-step model of the process of implementing a parallel learning structure. In Chapter 8, we step back from the mechanics of parallel learning structures to look at the ways in which they accomplish learning and change in organizations. We'll use experiential learning theory as a basis for understanding why learning gets blocked in organizations and what needs to be done to overcome that. As well, we will describe seven different "metaphors of change" and link them to changes we observed in the cases.

2

Pursuing Efficiency and Innovation Simultaneously

Contingency theory in organization design basically asserts that in a stable environment the best thing to do is organize for efficiency, and in an uncertain environment, organize for innovation. This is seen as a basic trade-off; organizational characteristics that lead to innovation are the opposite of those that lead to efficiency. Studies of long-term organizational effectiveness, however, reveal that it is possible to be both efficient and innovative.[1] Recognition of that—and the vision of simultaneous learning (innovation) and striving (efficiency)—are resulting in numerous experiments in organization design.[2] The use of a parallel learning structure coupled with a more conventional organizational design may be one way of accomplishing this vision.

Case: Intercon Semiconductor

Intercon Semiconductor was founded in 1961 and was one of the first companies to manufacture integrated circuits exclusively. The

Text on pages 20–23 is reprinted by permission from Shani/Elliot, "Applying Sociotechnical System Design at the Strategic Apex: An Illustration," *Organization Development Journal*, Vol. 6, No. 2, Summer 1988. © 1988 by the Organization Development Institute.

1. For example, Pascale and Athos (1981), Lawrence and Dyer (1983).

2. For example, Semco's organization design (Semler, 1989), Stratified Systems Theory (Jaques, 1989).

company's evolution resulted in six product-line divisions and two specific market divisions. Each division designed, manufactured, and marketed its own products. The company was headquartered on the East coast with five additional production facilities throughout the United States and overseas. By 1982, Intercon had 13,000 employees and had grown since 1972 at a compounded annual growth rate of 26 percent (excluding the 1981–82 recession), outpacing industry growth by 7 percent. Revenues in 1983 were $600 million, and were projected to triple by 1988. However, the 1985 industry recession resulted in revenues of $400 million. By 1988, Intercon had rebounded and had over 9,000 employees, making it one of the largest companies in the semiconductor industry.

The American semiconductor industry emerged in the field of electronics in 1952 when integrated circuit (IC) technology became the foundation of the entire electronics sector. From its inception, the industry has been characterized by innovative entrepreneurialism. This entrepreneurialism created a turbulent, uncertain, and competitive environment. By 1972, there were 289 companies in the industry. The average annual industry growth rate in the sixties and the seventies was over 13 percent. This trend continued through 1984. The availability of venture capital enabled the creation of new companies as "spin-offs" of existing companies so that by 1985, 414 separate companies within the semiconductor industry had been established.[3] The industry is capital-intensive and highly sensitive to market fluctuations because it is based largely on derived demand —most devices are sold to original equipment manufacturers. Technological advantage has been extremely important but difficult to maintain. Interfirm mobility of scientists and engineers and long delays between innovation and patent protection are contributing factors. While the normal development cycle for major new products used to be longer than two years, the pressure to develop new and more complex ICs quickly has forced companies to adopt "less-than-year" planning and product development time frames. Stiff competition, stagnating markets, and increasingly high research and capital costs hit hard at the U. S. industry.

---

3. Schoonhoven (1986).

Background to the Intervention

In 1985 Intercon Semiconductor faced shrinking markets and increased competition from abroad in production effectiveness, efficiency, pricing, and product innovation. In response, the company devoted significant resources toward reorganization. In August 1985, Intercon announced a zero defects warranty on all of its semiconductor products. It was the first IC company to offer the warranty. The zero defects warranty was the result of several years of attempts to improve quality control that had begun in 1979.[4] In 1979, a defect level of one per thousand had been accepted. By 1985, a number of the previous defects had been totally eliminated. Results of this program had, however, been uneven.

In 1986, the President of Intercon was looking for ways to foster both efficiency and innovation in the company. The Vice-President for Human Resources Management and Strategy, with input from the senior executive group, formed a nine-member steering committee of managers to guide and oversee the effort. Members were chosen so that, collectively, the steering committee had a broad view and understanding of the entire organization. Figure 2.1 presents the Intercon organizational chart and highlights the steering-committee members' home bases. Three off-site meetings of the steering committee with internal and external consultants resulted in a detailed proposal to the executive group of the company. They proposed a system-wide assessment of Intercon based on sociotechnical systems (STS) theory and using a parallel learning structure as the means for accomplishing the assessment.[5]

Parallel Structure Creation

The steering committee's proposal was presented at a meeting of the executive group by the three members of the steering committee who were also part of the executive team. At this meeting a shared understanding of the company's needs for increased innovation and efficiency was developed. The fit between the proposed project's

---

4. This process was based on Crosby's (1979) work.

5. For more detail on sociotechnical systems theory, please refer to Appendix A and the theory section in Chapter 6. More on the use of STS by executives can be found in Shani and Elliott (1988).

Figure 2.1
Intercon Semiconductor organization chart showing the positions of steering-committe-members

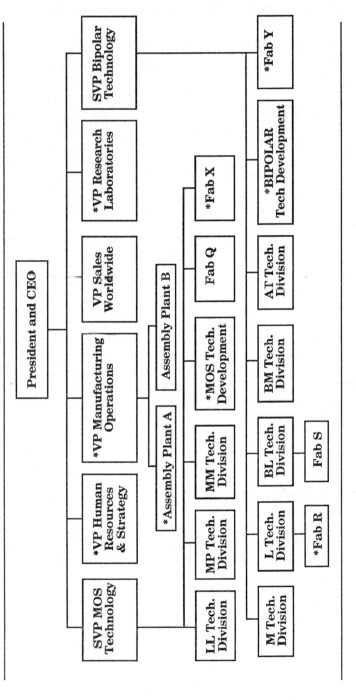

* Denotes steering-committee member. All units were represented on either the ideas committee, the action committee, or both.

vision and the company's vision, and the underlying philosophy of the proposal were extensively discussed. The quality of the discussion was enhanced by the executive group's partial familiarity with both STS and parallel learning structures. The newest manufacturing facility had been built using STS design principles. The zero defects quality improvement program had been implemented through a modified parallel structure that was still in existence throughout the organization. The mixed experience with the quality improvement effort and the perceived similarity to the parallel learning structure created some confusion and skepticism, however. The "Quality Improvement Organization" (as this parallel structure was called) had a "quality council" (i.e., a steering committee) that reported to the CEO and oversaw and managed many "quality improvement teams" throughout the corporation. As proposed, the parallel learning structure would have a steering committee (that would report to the executive group) and two action groups. As the discussion progressed, distinct roles and boundary definitions of the parallel learning structure were devised:

1. The parallel learning structure would be a microcosm of the entire corporation; it would be large enough to be representative of the organization but small enough to be manageable.

2. The parallel structure would be composed of three groups:

   a) a steering committee to oversee and guide the project,

   b) an action committee to conduct the organizational assessment and explore options for operational redesign, and

   c) an ideas committee to foster creative brainstorming within and outside the parallel learning structure.

The last part of the meeting was devoted to the identification of criteria and procedures for the formation of the action and ideas committees and the establishment of an interface and reporting mechanism between the parallel learning structure and the executive group.

Divisional and plant managers throughout the organization were asked to recommend employees for both committees. Following a screening process that focused on people's levels of expertise, the steering committee notified the managers of their choices. Managers discussed the project with the organizational members and attempted to enlist their voluntary commitment to take part in the endeavor. At that point, it was estimated that people would have to spend 25 percent of their time on this project.

A short letter from the CEO to the organizational members announcing the new project's charter and briefly describing the parallel learning structure's design and operation was followed by an off-site meeting of the newly formed parallel learning structure. The meeting was opened by the CEO, who emphasized the importance of the project. The Chair of the steering committee reviewed the evolution of the project to date, its charter, and its potential duration. Two and a half days of a basic STS workshop and team-building activities followed. The last half day was devoted to the devolopment of an action plan for an overall organizational assessment, later approved by the executive group.

Inquiry Phase

The development of the actual data-collection tools, (i.e., interview guides, surveys, technical and task analysis guides, and methods for environmental analysis) and the actual data collection lasted four months. At first the ideas group didn't quite know what to do with itself. To get it started, development of the data-collection instruments was divided between the study group (which took initial responsibility for the development of the interview guides and the survey) and the ideas group (which took initial responsibility for the development of the technical and environmental guides). Each group had the opportunity to carefully review the instruments that were developed by the other group. The steering committee reviewed all the instruments. After that, the study group did the actual data collection and data analysis. Once an initial analysis of the data was complete, the ideas group became very active in facilitating creative solution meetings for the parallel structure and in developing recommendations for change. Both groups collaborated in preparing a report for the executive group. Approximately six months after the parallel structure was launched, the report was presented to the executive group. Following is a brief descriptive summary of the findings that were presented to the executive committee.

Business Situation. The industry was seen as increasingly competitive, with customers demanding innovative, high-quality products, and just-in-time production schedules. Moreover, the Japanese continued to gain market share. During the down cycles, Japanese firms continued to add capacity in preparation for quick up-turns. Furthermore, Japanese firms were spending a proportionately larger percentage of sales on research and development.

Business Strategy. There was an overall sense of frustration with the entire strategic-planning process. The four-year planning cycle used by the company seemed unrealistic, given the broad swings in the industry which no one seemed to be able to predict. There was cynicism and skepticism about the "numbers game" and a believable vision of where the company was going had not been articulated. Talk of innovation in certain areas was not matched by results, nor was there a sense of urgency about new products. There was no agreement about what the company's strategic and competitive competencies were. Product-development plans tended not to support each other across divisions and sometimes even within divisions. In general, the feeling was that the company needed to be more market-driven rather than product- or technology-driven and clearly had to focus on the emerging "semicustom" market.

Decision Making. There were many committees, councils, and groups that focused on tactical issues. Not enough time was spent on the strategic issues, especially at the corporate staff level. The hard questions about the business were not asked, and division managers felt that they did not have enough input on matters pertaining to their own business. Important issues got buried in the bureaucratic process and remained unresolved. Meanwhile, the competitors seemed to be gaining the edge in responding to customers as the company's own bureaucracy stifled attempts to do things differently.

Information Systems. The demands for detailed information that came from the corporate office were seen as excessive and made work difficult: "Too much of not the right kind of data fills the in-baskets and jams the system."

Technical System. The company's product lines were associated with particular technologies. However, these technologies were beginning to merge in more complex and integrated new products, which created problems of charter and identity for the existing product divisions. Furthermore, it was not clear whether the company was investing in the right technologies for the future.

Structure. The fabrication of wafers (chips) had been decentralized within product divisions so that, on the whole, each division had control of its own fab area. Yet, in almost every division, some of their products were being made in someone else's fab area because of the overlapping technologies and increasingly complex chips. While it was clear that important economies of scale could be achieved through centralized fabrication, it was unclear whether centralized manufacturing would facilitate or impede the innovation process. Turf battles between divisions in different product/technology groups were becoming more prominent, and a controversy was heating up over whether groups should be formed around markets rather than technology.

Social System. There was a very positive assessment of the talent of the people in the company, but at the same time a belief that the company had not yet capitalized on that talent. There was a sense of cooperation and willingness to work together, yet the skills to develop teamwork were lacking, especially in middle management, and were not demonstrated by top management, either. There was technical depth, but a lack of managerial depth. The cyclical nature of the business also brought high turnover in management, and with that, different and constantly changing views of how the organization should be put together. The quality improvement program had been the single most important thing to alter the culture of the company in the past four years. There was still, however, a deep-seated lack of identity.

Reward and Control Systems. There was a general feeling that despite the performance-based reward/bonus system, the company had a history of being easy on people and still paying off when things didn't get done; this was especially true in the area of new products, where milestones were continually missed. Some felt that managers too often compromised in their statement of performance objectives at the expense of making the right decision for the business.

Business Results. The company was seen as being oriented more toward procedures than results. Overall, the company had not been as successful as it could be in getting new products out and had been too dependent on old technology. The company was not successful enough in developing new products. In addition, there was a sense that the company did not have a winning culture, or the sense of urgency that was required in an increasingly competitive marketplace. There was a lack of responsiveness to the market, and some managers believed that the firm was too frequently treated as a second source for its long-term health.

The report was initially tabled at a regular executive group meeting by the two executives who were also steering-committee members. Then a whole day was set aside for an off-site meeting to deliberate the parallel learning structure's findings and to discuss their potential implications. The meeting involved only the executive group and the steering committee. Following a review of the data-collection and data-analysis processes, a summary of the findings was presented. In some areas, raw data and graphs were shared. Management made a sincere attempt to understand the data, the findings, and their potential meaning. Executives were highly impressed (some were quite surprised) with the quality and depth of the analysis. The meeting concluded with the executive group directing the parallel learning structure to generate alternative sets of recommendations that would position the company to compete in a market that demanded increasingly complex innovations and significant cost reductions. (A sudden downturn within the semiconductor industry had put pressure on Intercon to reduce costs.)

Actions Emanating from the Inquiry

Due to time pressure from the executive group and the need to divide labor efficiently, the steering committee, in collaboration with the two groups, decided that the action committee would focus on alternative designs to increase efficiency and the ideas committee would focus on alternative designs to increase innovation. While many alternative design ideas were generated by both teams, finding the middle-range alternatives that would optimize both innovation and efficiency was an overwhelming task. The best design alternative for fostering innovation was the worst in its potential impact on efficiency. Similarly, the best design alternative for efficiency would foster limited innovation, at best. As a result of these discrepancies, a significant amount of conflict was building up within the parallel learning structure. A two-day, off-site meeting of the entire parallel learning structure was held that focused on finding the appropriate balance between how to best promote innovation while exploiting every opportunity to increase efficiency.

After considerable deliberations, the parallel learning structure worked out three options of alternative restructuring of the company. One was potentially a little better for increasing efficiency, one a little better for fostering innovation, and the third one aimed more at the middle range. The executive group chose the middle-ranged alternative, and with some minor modifications, implemented the design four weeks later.

The essence of the redesign involved stripping the major product groups of their technological differences and reconfiguring into what might best be described as groups differentiated by a greater orientation to commodity versus highly innovative products. This allowed for more focus on the semicustom market and made the basically product-oriented divisions more discernible to customers. A second change was in the number of divisions. The absolute number of divisions was reduced from eight to five in an effort to achieve economies of scale and thus accommodate the pressure to radically reduce costs.

The technology-development groups, which were previously separated within the two product groups, were combined within R & D as part of the reorientation of technology toward new products that combined the heretofore separate technologies. This centralization resulted in some economies of scale and responded to the merging of technologies embodied in the new divisional structure. The R & D group itself was to become far more oriented toward specific research areas defined by the market opportunities as opposed to those defined more by technological breakthroughs.

While these changes allowed for more efficient use of resources and faster product-development life cycles, they did not respond to the need for a more flexible, adaptive organization. It was recognized that more changes to the organization itself might be needed in the near future. In a surprise move, the executive group institutionalized the parallel learning structure as an integral part of the organization. It has become a built-in mechanism for ongoing organizational transformation. The only change to the original design was the establishment of a procedure for rotating members in and out of the parallel structure. Every six months, one-third of the members of each committee (i.e., steering, action, and ideas) are rotated out, while new organizational members are brought on board.

As this case is written in late 1988, the parallel learning structure is involved with the following tasks:

1. They are exploring alternative organizational designs for moving beyond the linear, sequential process of new-product development (moving from functional group to functional group) toward some form of reciprocal, or simultaneous, development method. The purpose is to reduce overall development time and build commitment to new-product development.

2. The information system is undergoing examination with the purpose of quickly generating and disseminating usable data to relevant functional groups.

3. The reward system, and entire value system, of the company are being examined to find ways of incorporating a new sense of urgency into the product-development effort. In this, the importance of the existing and successful quality program has been affirmed and the program is being restrengthened and reexamined for ideas on how to facilitate functional interfaces critical to the new "simultaneous product development" process.

The change efforts described above are happening in the midst of layoffs and tremendous short-term survival pressures. The strategic repositioning of the company is not yet complete, although major changes in internal design have already occurred. The company has not been able to develop a completely thought-out master design, and that may be impossible to do in a fast-paced and volatile environment. With the parallel learning structure as a transformation mechanism, however, changes are being made in discrete "chunks" to optimize the fit among the strategic, technical, and social systems, while attending to increases in efficiency and innovation.

Analysis and Some Learnings from the Case

In this section, we'll look at the Intercon case mainly in terms of structural issues in designing for efficiency and innovation and the parallel learning structure's utility as a mechanism for ongoing organizational adaptation. At Intercon, the parallel learning structure became a mechanism for ongoing innovation in the very fabric of the organization itself. We'll also look at one other parallel learning structure design that is more geared to supporting individual innovation in large bureaucracies.

Designing for Efficiency, Innovation, and Organizational Adaptation

The ability of an organization to adapt itself to changing environmental conditions is a result of many things. Here we'll focus on the impact of organizational structure. In general, structures that result in efficient organization make it difficult for the organization to change and adapt. Structures that result in innovation and change require considerable slack and tolerance of inefficiencies.[6] So there exists a basic dilemma, as those at Intercon clearly found out.

The most efficient organization requires competent execution of well-designed work routines with a minimum of waste. Such organizations routinize as much work as possible and search for ever better routines to do more with less. This is efficient because rules and routines act as the means for coordinating labor. Having to meet face-to-face to coordinate work is very costly. With routines, everyone becomes a specialist in his or her small domain and all the pieces eventually fit together. These organizations, however, require a fair degree of stability in their product base, customers, and competitors. Routinization reduces organizational adaptability for a number of reasons. First, it precludes innovative acts from those whose work is routinized. In addition, it tends to ossify the organization because when there is a high level of interdependence between various work routines, changing one means that many others must be changed as well. Finally, people develop loyalties to some routines, which makes it all the more difficult to change the routines when necessary. In efficient organizations, adaptation is driven by strategic changes made at the top, and it requires long planning cycles and lead times.

If the rate of change in the environment precludes the use of routinization for efficiency, then other means of fostering maximum

---

6. Efficiency is simply the ratio of inputs to outputs. Innovation is the adoption of a change, either self-initiated or imitated.

output from minimum effort and resources are needed. Centralization, functional grouping, direct supervision (hierarchy), goal setting, and tight reporting and control systems are some of the design attributes that can foster efficiency. At Intercon, the planners decided to increase centralization (fewer divisions) and functionally group their R & D resources. They were also working toward clarifying their product-development goals.

All of these ways of improving efficiency share the attributes of increasing organizational control and concentrating attention and effort toward some predetermined outcome. Having to attend to too many shifting priorities at once precludes the possibility of efficient performance. Peak-performance psychology in sports, and its application to management training, is based on the principle of focused concentration. This psychology supports the point of view that organizations should strive to "buffer their operating cores from uncertainty" and leave the adaptation to senior managers. With a moderate rate of environmental change, planning can still work as an adaptation mechanism, but planning cycles and lead times need to be considerably shortened.

There are some problems with planning from the top as the key adaptation mechanism. First, when organizational members aren't involved in the planning (especially key line managers, like the divisional and plant managers at Intercon), it creates resistance to implementation. When operating cores are buffered from the pressure of the environment, unrealistic perspectives and expectations develop. Many will be unaware of the environmental pressures demanding adaptation and therefore unresponsive to plans formulated at the top. Another reason for resistance comes from the quality of the plans themselves. Those at the top are bound to be ignorant of local conditions and the complexities faced by people actually doing the work.

Furthermore, planning at the top has its own inefficiencies in that it does not use the talent and knowledge of employees who are working at the boundaries of the organization and therefore are involved daily with the organization's relevant environments. Top-down planning is too laborious to work when the rate of environmental change is too fast for conventional planning cycles, like it was at Intercon. Decentralizing organizations to allow for semiautonomous units that can more easily adapt to their local conditions increases adaptability, but reduces the efficiencies that come from centralized economies of scale and functional grouping. The question is how best to retain the efficiencies of formal organization while adding an adaptive capacity.

Intercon's Parallel Learning Structure: Increasing Organizational Adaptation

Intercon's parallel learning structure is a promising approach for achieving continuous organizational innovation and adaptation. In this design, there is a distinct structure with a specific division and coordination of labor (i.e., the steering committee, the action committee, the ideas committee) that operates side-by-side and is strongly linked to the formal hierarchy and structure of the operating organization (i.e., three members of the steering committee are also members of the executive group, the members of the parallel learning structure are collectively not only a microcosm of the operating organization but are also members of the formal organization). The parallel learning structure's purpose is to scan the organization and its environment and continuously look for ways to improve organizational functioning. The formal organization can then be structured to fully optimize the qualities needed for efficient performance.

In the Intercon case, operating in a parallel mode with a clearly defined structure permitted the parallel learning structure to provide an arena for ongoing dialogue about the current state of the organization. It utilized the knowledge, contacts, and expertise of organizational members who normally would not gain access to arenas for strategic planning. The fact that the parallel learning structure was designed to be a *microcosm* was especially important in ensuring that all relevant aspects of the organization were taken into account. The ongoing dialogue within the parallel learning structure and between the parallel learning structure members and those in the formal organization resulted not only in an accurate understanding of the organization's current state but also in an insightful set of ideas for organizational redesign in order to realign Intercon with its current environment.

The ideas group played a key role in fostering adaptation and change within and outside the parallel learning structure. Internally, it shared some of the responsibility and workload during the development of the data-collection method, challenged the data-collection tools developed by the study group, worked through sorting out the data, and worked at being creative around the interpretation of the data. The ideas group also took responsibility for facilitating many of the brainstorming sessions of the entire parallel learning structure that focused on the development of recommendations for adaptation and change. One of this group's most important attributes was how it was perceived by other employees. A few of the group's members were perceived as very talented but eccentric innovators who usually did not pay any attention to authority and status. Because these "crazies" were involved in the parallel structure, other employees believed that the executive group was really sincere about change and that something creative and different might actually emerge from the effort.

The computer industry is known for high innovation (and low efficiency) and, no doubt, these characteristics applied to Intercon in its early, entrepreneurial years. What seemed to have happened was that a sort of complacency set in, and along with it, an increased emphasis on efficiency. In the Intercon case, the parallel structure was not only a structural intervention, but a cultural one. Indeed, its main initial effect may have been to provide focus to a necessary cultural change.

The decision by the executive group to institutionalize the parallel learning structure with the rotation procedure has a number of implications. One is that the rotation system will enhance the diffusion of cultural change throughout the organization. Second, it helps to link the parallel learning structure more closely with the formal organization. Third, it ensures an ongoing supply of new "blood" into the innovating part of the organization.

At Intercon, the parallel structure is not looked to as a source of innovation in product design or marketing. Rather, it has been directed to examine and propose ongoing modifications to the organization as a whole in order to continually realign the system with its environment. But parallel learning structures can be designed to foster intrapreneurial innovation, as described in the next section.

Using Parallel Learning Structures to Foster Innovation in Highly Efficient Organizations

Some organizations, like mass-production manufacturing, must maintain high levels of efficiency to remain viable. As mentioned above, structural attributes that foster efficiency routinize work and focus energy and attention on predetermined outcomes.

Innovation, however, requires being open to new, unplanned outcomes and attending to the novel and unexpected. Most of the attributes of efficient organizing create barriers to innovation. Similarly, structures that foster innovation—for example, decentralization and small, self-contained, self-regulating units—generally result in less efficiency. This dilemma has been acknowledged by researchers and managers alike.[7] Attempts to overcome the formal organization's limited ability to foster innovation have made it clear that the task of the innovating organization is somewhat different from that of the operating organization. Some recent experiments include the "skunkworks," or "dual" organization, and the "new-venture unit."

In its original form, a "skunkworks" was the unsanctioned creation of a maverick manager with an idea and a passion to pursue it who could convince others to bootleg resources and work on the idea. As it has come to be formalized, the skunkworks, or the dual organization, is set up as an entirely separate division of groups charged with innovation as their task, complete discretion on funding, and autonomy on how to manage the task.[8] Such groups usually report directly to the senior executive or executive team. The procedures, policies, and organizational processes of the formal organization do not apply to the dual organization. This is not much different from the case of a separate and specialized R & D unit, and it recreates many of R & D's problems. One major challenge for management is learning how to create and foster integration between the dual organization and the operating organization. A second challenge is learning how to maintain the innovative thrust as the dual organization increases in size.

New-venture units refer to small groups that are charged with innovation but are not organized into a separate division.[9] These groups are usually physically separated in special research centers and may be individually funded, but are formally part of the operating organization. As such, most of the formal organization's policies and procedures apply to the units. The major challenge for management is fostering innovative behavior in a relatively bureaucratic setting. Early evidence suggests that few successful innovations are engendered by this design.[10]

---

7. E.g., Duncan (1976), Daft (1978).

8. Galbraith (1982).

9. Acar, Melcher, and Aupperle (1987).

10. Bart (1988).

Parallel learning structures have the potential to overcome the limitations of these other designs. Because parallel structure members are also members of the formal organization, linkage between the two may not be as difficult to maintain. Yet, the policies, norms, and operating procedures of the parallel learning structure are different from those of the formal organization and promote learning and innovation.

One design that is currently being experimented with looks well suited for encouraging individual initiative and innovative acts. It involves the use of a permanent steering committee with temporary action groups that form and disband around projects initiated by the people forming the groups. In this design, the steering committee is composed of senior managers who control key resources in the system, especially money and people's time. Anybody in the organization can propose a project to the steering committee. The steering committee then either turns down or agrees to the project. If it agrees, it commits to resource the project adequately and gives project team members a specified time off work to meet in their parallel structure groups. The groups initiate and implement their innovations, and then disband.

What this design does is preserve the efficiencies of the formal organization while creating a time and space for individuals to pursue innovative ideas. It also has the potential to increase the amount of networking and interunit linking within the formal organization. Rigid boundaries within efficient organizations create barriers to innovation because new and useful ideas often require integrating the knowledge of different functions. To the extent that groups are formed with representatives of different functions relevant to the project, this parallel learning structure can help overcome the problems of isolation that plague innovation in organizations.

This kind of parallel learning structure not only overcomes some of the structural barriers to innovation, but also can create the kind of organizational climate within bureaucracies that will encourage individuals to take initiatives.[11] In the first place, it increases the individual's opportunities to be assigned challenging, growth-enhancing tasks, thereby increasing individual motivation

---

11. The following is adapted from Kanter (1983).

and energy. Second, it increases individual power and influence by opening up access to information, resources, support, and visibility. When people feel more powerful in their organizations, their commitment and their effectiveness increase as well. Some authors argue that organizational adaptability comes less from organizational structure and more from individual initiatives, particularly in the middle and bottom ranks of an organization. Individual initiatives require motivation, influence, and the development of supporting groups to sustain the development and implementation of innovations. This parallel learning structure design appears to provide a place in highly efficient organizations where such supportive groups can be formed and helps to generate the conditions that lead to motivation and influence for those in the middle and at the bottom.

Key Points in Using Parallel Learning Structures to Increase Organizational Adaptation

1. At the formation stage of the parallel learning structure establish clear role boundaries between the steering, action, and ideas committees. Helping the groups develop a distinct identity via some team-building activities fosters task efficiency and a feeling of accomplishment at the formation stage of the parallel learning structure.

2. Having at least two members of the executive group be on the steering committee is crucial for the project's perceived legitimacy. It also aids in developing an ongoing interface with the executive group and helps ensure their input.

3. Ensuring that the parallel learning structure is a microcosm of the complete organization will provide the necessary flow of information from all levels and parts of the organization. The ongoing dialogue between the parallel learning structure members and their peers about their activities and a continuous solicitation of input will also reduce the resistance to changes that are likely to result from the effort.

4. Equalization of power and influence between the action and ideas groups is an area that requires specific atten-

tion. The consultants have to make sure that the groups use their potential and avoid getting into an ongoing competition or power struggle. Ways of reducing inevitable intergroup competition must be found. The more distinct the group's tasks are, the less competitive they tend to be. But watch out for signs that one group wants to be "better" than another.

5. The rotation of members between the parallel learning structure groups and the formal organization will enhance the legitimacy of the structure and facilitate the introduction of innovation. It will also enhance the capacity of the parallel learning structure to generate new ideas continuously.

3

Solving Problems Bureaucracies Cannot Handle

A host of relentless pressures are forcing health care institutions (HCIs) to undergo a complex, confusing set of difficult changes. A partial list of industry-wide issues includes deinstitutionalization, rising expectations regarding medical care, cost containment, escalating medical costs, and regulations. HCIs are being pushed at once toward rapid consolidation into large, multihospital corporations or systems, and toward the development of internal coping and response mechanisms.

HCIs possess organizational features that are distinctly different from other business and industrial organizations. The way "bottom line" success or failure is determined in a manufacturing organization is ill-suited to an organization devoted to health care delivery. Moreover, in goods-producing organizations, work redesign, system redesign, quality of work life projects, and other employee involvement and organizational improvement strategies can be justified on the basis of documented increases in productivity. In human-service organizations, nonprofit settings, and HCIs, on the other hand, the application of standard measures of productivity

Portions of this chapter are reprinted by permission from Shani/Eberhardt, "Parallel Organizations in a Health Care Institution," *Group & Organization Studies,* Vol. 12, No. 2, June 1987, pp. 147–173. © Sage Publications, Inc.

and performance raises a host of organizational problems.[1] Since the main objective of an HCI is to provide professional individualized care, and treatment is rendered directly to the client by specialists according to the needs and requirements of each case, much of the work in the system cannot be mechanized, standardized, or pre-planned.[2] The work and organizational design of the HCI needs to respond to more uncertain and complex issues than is the case with machine bureaucracies whose principal output is a physical product.

Another feature that distinguishes HCIs from other organizations is the dual hierarchy of medical and administrative authority. Not only are hospital managers operating under unique managerial constraints in mobilizing their resources, but the physicians, who are often beyond the administrators' control, are the ones who determine both how and to what extent the HCI is actually used. Furthermore, the physicians have the resources (financial and human skills) to compete in their own offices with many hospital services. As a result, many physicians have limited interest in improvement of the overall functioning of the HCI.[3] These distinctive characteristics of HCIs, as well as their bureaucratic complexity, are some of the formidable barriers to improving their operating effectiveness. Another factor is the health care industry's historical difficulty in responding to environmental pressures for change.

Case: Grate Hospital

Located in the Midwest and serving a population of about 100,000 residents, Grate Hospital is a 100-bed medical rehabilitation facility with about 700 outpatients. The center employs approximately 450 personnel, of whom 150 are part-time employees. Although it is a state-affiliated facility, associated with the state university, it is self-funded. The Executive Director, the Dean of the University Medical School, together with the Medical Director and Hospital Administrator, are charged with the responsibility of managing the center. Two major subsystems, with their own mix of people, tasks,

---

1. Goldsmith (1980), Margulies and Adams (1982).

2. Georgopoulos (1981).

3. Weisbord and Stoelwinder (1979).

managerial values, and styles, coexist at Grate: the medical group that provides the medical services and the administrative, maintenance group that provides the support services. Thirteen professional departments, which compose the medical subsystem, serve as the human resources core out of which clinical teams for health care delivery are created. The clinical teams, composed of professional staff members, are formed on the basis of individual patient needs. A formal team leader is designated and responsible for coordinating the treatment of the patient.

Initial Entry

During the design and delivery of a basic supervision course, a number of discrepancies surfaced in the way these clinical teams operated. For example, in some of the teams the formal team leader was a physician (M.D.), while in others a case manager functioned as team leader. Management's past attempts at standardizing clinical team functioning resulted in very little success; some of the physicians never agreed to relinquish their role as the leaders. When the dynamics within the teams were carefully examined, it became apparent that how the teams actually functioned was different from the philosophy espoused by top management. Furthermore, there was a lot of variety in the work processes, structures, and procedures used by different teams.

Senior managers believed that clinical team functioning was a key factor in overall hospital effectiveness. They felt that the time had come to address the issues of team design, leadership, and procedures. Past attempts to do this unilaterally had failed. They believed that a different approach to "solving" the problem of how to best deliver team care was necessary.

The consultants who taught the basic supervision course were approached by the Medical Director for an initial discussion of the challenge faced by top management. They suggested the hospital use an action-research study housed within a parallel learning structure to address the structure and process of effective team health care delivery.

Parallel Structure Creation

The Medical Director championed the project and helped create a nine-member steering committee for the parallel learning structure. With the consultants, the steering committee defined the initial boundaries, scope, and potential next steps in the creation of the parallel structure and developed the criteria and procedures for the selection of the parallel structure's members. They decided to set up a "study group," composed as follows:

1. Representatives of each of the medical professional departments
2. Employees whose length of tenure at Grate was representative of the employee population at large
3. Employees who were at least moderately verbal and who would be perceived as representative by their constituents
4. Employees who agreed voluntarily to serve on the study group

Employees were suggested by managers and informally approached to test out their willingness to get involved. Those who seemed willing were officially notified of their appointment. A schematic illustration of Grate Hospital's formal organization and the parallel learning structure that was created is presented in Fig. 3.1.

The first, formal meeting of the entire parallel learning structure included all the steering-committee and study-group members as well as the consultants. The meeting was held away from the hospital at an off-site location and was led by the Medical Director. After a review of the agenda and an explanation of the expectations for the meeting, the Chair of the steering committee described the evolution of the project, its potential duration, and the criteria that were used in selecting study-group members. The consultants, after being introduced, described the action-research philosophy and the parallel learning structure's operating procedures. The functions and initial tasks of the three subgroups (steering committee, study group, and consultants) within the parallel structure were discussed. While ample time was allowed for members to ask clarifying questions, most of the concerns were related to procedural matters. The first meeting ended with a role-expectations and role-negotiation exercise. Each of the three groups (steering, study, and consulting) met separately to discuss what they felt their role and responsibilities were and what expectations they held for the other two groups. These were recorded on flip-chart paper, and then each group presented its deliberations. A lively discussion followed that clarified expectations and helped to establish clear role identities within the newly formed parallel learning structure.

Figure 3.1
Grate Hospital and its parallel learning structure

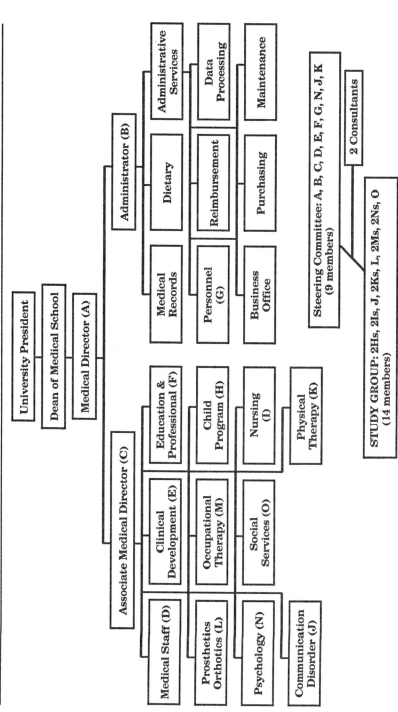

Early Problems

Although the initial meetings were focused on creating a strong identity for the parallel learning structure, it took some time for boundaries to get established. In the early meetings of the study group, members were pessimistic and couldn't shake a sense of powerlessness. Two members of the study group, who served as a liaison between the study group and the steering committee (and who were also senior managers in the hospital), had to absorb a lot of hostility from some members of the study group about management's past reluctance and unresponsiveness to suggestions for improvements. The comments, "Why, now, will it be any different?" "How committed is management to making changes?" and "Let's send up a balloon and see if it flies!" exemplify the initial atmosphere that existed within the parallel structure. The role of the liaison persons became critical.

The consultants met alone twice with the liaison people after two hostile meetings. During these sessions the two managers and the consultants jointly explored the reasons for people's hostility and came to understand that the confrontations were not personally directed at these managers. The consultants worked with the liaison persons and the steering committee so that they were able to hear the anger, anxiety, and hopelessness of the employees. They developed an understanding of the process's internal dynamics and kept faith in their ability to manage the project.

Subsequently, the consultants facilitated two meetings between the study group and the steering committee to work out the study group's issues. As the meetings progressed, the steering committee and the liaison people learned to respond less defensively and to focus on the content of the issues that were raised. The acknowledgment by a physician, who was a member of the study group, that many of the problems rested with some physicians' behavior helped reduce a great deal of tension and led to the development of a more constructive atmosphere. For the first time, some real commitment to the project emerged.

Inquiry Phase

Out of these discussions between the steering committee and study group the need to "identify the key issues that influence the quality of team health care delivery" emerged as the focus of the project.

Different methods of inquiry were explored by the study group, and a multiphase plan was developed.

1. The members of the study group would conduct initial interviews of randomly selected organizational members.
2. They would then compile the themes that emerged from the initial interviews.
3. They would distribute to the entire organization a preliminary "issue survey," which would be used for prioritizing team issues.
4. A summary by the consultants of the results of the interviews and the initial issue survey would be fed back to the parallel learning structure, which would then interpret the data and attempt to develop a shared understanding of the results.
5. There would be focused study and action planning.

When organizational members were approached by the members of the study group for initial interviews, it became clear that those beyond the study group knew very little about the project. By that time, three different memos about the project and its evolution had been distributed to all Grate Hospital employees, but that had obviously not been sufficient. The act of interviewing some people, however, made the project much more visible.

The study group compiled the issues associated with team health care delivery into a preliminary survey for all hospital employees to prioritize. The turbulent events to follow were foreshadowed when the steering committee received a hostile letter from one of the physicians that stated, "These are not the issues that we should be concerned with . . . the study in its present focus and format is worthless . . . ." While the steering committee chose to ignore the letter, the consultants worked with the parallel learning structure to improve the flow of information between the parallel learning structure and the formal organization. Political tensions were not addressed at this time.

Based on the results from hospital members' prioritization of the issues associated with "the quality of health care team delivery" all members of the parallel learning structure concluded that the clinical teams' work dynamics needed to be further examined. Parallel learning structure members were given some training in participant-observation techniques and charged with the responsibility to record their observations.

Concurrently, the study group and the consultants developed a questionnaire with 114 questions covering the attitudes and perceptions of the clinical team process and its organizational context, hospital and departmental characteristics, the features of the varied medical disciplines, team work design, team leaders' management style, communication process, decision-making process, the nature of working conditions, identification with the team, team effectiveness, general satisfaction, and demographics. The questionnaire was announced by a letter from the steering committee Chair and completion was strictly voluntary.

The participant-observation activity was announced in a memo and at a general staff meeting that included all the physicians. As study group members began systematic observations some of the tensions surfaced. For example, one of the physicians who led a clinical team meeting asked the study group member who was supposed to observe the meeting to leave the room because he (the physician) did not believe the study was worthwhile and he thought the aims of the study were meaningless. This study group member immediately confronted the Medical Director, who was supposed to have secured the physician's acceptance. The Medical Director in turn confronted the physician, who then apologized to the observer at the next clinical team meeting with the statement, "Although I am still skeptical about this study, it is okay with me for you to observe the meeting." This was seen by the study group as the first time the Medical Director had really stood behind the group and the project. This, of course, resulted in a tremendous boost of energy and enthusiasm within the study group. A few attempts by people in the steering committee to meet later with this physician were unsuccessful; he managed to cancel three scheduled meetings. Overall, although tension existed within the system, both the questionnaire and the observations took place as planned.

Unanticipated Side-Effects

While physician resistance was anticipated at the outset, neither the parallel learning structure members, the consultants, nor the Medical Director anticipated that, as the parallel learning structure started to function more effectively, some of the top managers in the hospital would become threatened. As the steering-committee members shared updates on what was happening with the study in the regular, top-level management meetings, comments such as, "Are we really ready for a study like this one?" and, "Are we sure that this is what we were initially after?" were expressed. The parallel learning structure worked under the assumption that the primary interest of management was to improve the quality of health care delivery. Thus, it was unprepared for the conflict that erupted as the initial data were collected and shared between some of the managers, the study group, and some of the physicians. Much of the data first compiled by the parallel learning structure pointed toward problems traceable to physicians' behavior and the administrators'/managers' styles. In addition to top management's defensiveness about its own part in the "problem," they were also very concerned about physician opposition. Senior managers worried that they had very little influence over the physicians, and some physicians threatened to leave if the study continued. They claimed that the study was "creating turmoil" in the clinical teams, though no actual examples of team disruption were ever uncovered. It seems that many doctors knew from their own experience that some teams worked better than others, but they were threatened by the notion of losing control of the teams. Rumors that teams led by case managers were showing good results further fueled their fears. Though the parallel learning structure had been able to create for itself a climate of more openness, trust, and co-inquiry, a similar climate did not exist throughout the hospital (though anecdotes about changes in past patterns of relating began to surface at this time).

The relationship between some of the physicians and the parallel structure was never completely repaired; some of the administrators' early concerns about losing control of the situation had been realized (e.g., the parallel structure distributing and collecting data independently of administrative procedures), and some of the physicians' early concerns about losing control of the choice of team work design had been sharpened (e.g., outsiders as observers of the process). Their lingering mistrust of the process was always detectable by the study group. Nevertheless, the Medical Director felt that clinical team functioning had to improve, and he held fast. Both the physicians and the administrators eventually did listen to what the parallel learning structure had to say (for reasons discussed in the theory section) and began to take some action to seriously develop a standardized approach to team work (as specified below) and to create the context (structures, processes, and procedures) within which the teams could function optimally.

Diagnosis

The interview data indicated that, in the minds of hospital members, health care team effectiveness was due to both direct and indirect causes. The direct causes that employees felt were unquestionably associated with team effectiveness included attitudes toward working in teams, key team processes, and the team culture. Hospital members thought indirect causes explained why some teams were more effective than others. They felt that teams that had a shared set of expectations about what constitutes clinical work team procedures were more effective.

The key issue that emerged from all the data was a distinction between "interdisciplinary" team functioning and "multidisciplinary" team functioning.[4] In a *multidisciplinary team,* the efforts of each individual are discipline-oriented and, although they might impinge upon clients or activities dealt with by other disciplines, they approached their clients primarily as individual specialists. To operate in this setting, one need only have the skills necessary to succeed in one's own discipline. *Interdisciplinary teams* are also composed of individuals from different disciplines working toward a common goal. In this case, however, individuals need not only the skills of their own discipline, but also are responsible for the group effort on behalf of the activity or client involved. This was a crucial distinction at Grate because it meant the difference between responsibility for one's own function (e.g., accurate lab tests) versus responsibility for the whole outcome (i.e., healthy patients). In addition, interdisciplinary teams require members to have the skills necessary for effective group interaction.

While senior management espoused an interdisciplinary philosophy (and liked to believe that was what was going on in the hospital), all the data argued against the likelihood of interdisciplinary functioning taking place at Grate. Clinical team members within departments took a significantly greater professional interest in each other than in members from different departments and were

---

4. The following definitions are paraphrased from Melvin (1981).

uncomfortable critiquing the work of other departments. Interdisciplinary functioning would require team members to take a professional interest in all of their fellow members, not just those in their same department. Additionally, the orientation and training of new employees to the clinical team process was only marginally adequate. It appeared that interdisciplinary team functioning would demand an extensive orientation and training program. Eventually, the interview insights, observation data, and questionnaire results were used to develop a process model of team health care delivery. This model became the basis for dialogue among all hospital members concerning what the team health care delivery process entailed. A key proposition of the model was that without a common set of expectations, fully shared by team members, for how teams should function, team effectiveness suffers. This was controversial because, if true, a standardized method of team work would need to be developed.

Actions Emanating from the Diagnosis

Based on this model and all the collected data, the parallel learning structure eventually prepared a list of recommendations for potential changes, ranging from adjusting some minor procedures to changing all the teams into interdisciplinary teams and redesigning the management system to support the new team design.

The consultant team was asked to draw up different implementation scenarios. They offered three. The first plan called for hospital-wide redesign that would incorporate the suggestions made by the parallel learning structure in a massive change program. It was a comprehensive plan to create a new work environment based on the use of a unified, interdisciplinary team approach for the entire hospital, developed and reinforced by the medical, administrative, and professional staff.

The second plan involved piecemeal changes in response to the parallel learning structure's recommendations to be implemented based on priorities set forth by management. The second plan avoided the "hot potato" of work team design and, therefore, did not respond to the need to reduce discrepancies between expected and actual team functioning.

The third plan consisted mainly of a scientific, longitudinal experiment to assess and compare the effectiveness of the interdisciplinary and multidisciplinary teams prior to the hospital-redesign effort. The third plan was more conservative, more reflective of the existing system, and more readily executed. The Medical Director agreed in theory that hospital redesign (Plan 1) was superior, but he opted for Plan 3 because of his assessment that it would take a truly scientific, controlled experiment to convince some of his physicians and administrators of the benefits of any one approach to team work design and because of the lack of conclusive evidence in the reported literature on the relative advantages of interdisciplinary versus multidisciplinary health care teams.

Subsequently, the data from the study were fed back to hospital employees by both management and the study group members, along with a list of actions to be taken next. The parallel learning structure, with some assistance from the consultants, designed a longitudinal experiment to scientifically assess and compare the effectiveness of the two kinds of teams. The parallel learning structure was charged with the responsibility to carry out and monitor the experiment. As the "ideal teams" for the experiment were created, the consultants, before leaving the system, helped the steering committee identify the next phases that would follow the experimental phase. By that point, the hospital had acquired and developed some of the basic learning mechanisms needed to learn about itself by itself. The hospital now had the structure and the processes that could generate knowledge and recommendations for actions to overcome its own bureaucratic limitations.

Analysis and Some Learnings from the Case

This is a case of a very difficult and uneven application of a parallel structure strategy, and it highlights a number of the problems one is likely to run into when intervening in a system characterized by large power differentials, fragmentation, mistrust, and a history of antagonism. The parallel learning structure emerged out of the initial discussion between the consultants and the senior management of Grate Hospital as a suitable approach for a holistic understanding of the unique characteristics of team health care delivery. The organizational features, the participants' ideologies and political awareness, the quality of the working relationships that evolved, and the interface between the parallel learning structure and the formal organization influenced not only the developmental process of the parallel learning structure, but also its ability to fulfill its mission optimally.

Although it is impossible here to capture the full experience, development, and performance of the parallel structure, it can be said that the parallel learning structure was both successful and controversial in fulfilling its role. Even in early meetings, several members stated that they felt this was the first realistic approach to understanding and improving clinical team functioning the hospital had tried, and showed their enthusiasm through their hard work. Members of the parallel learning structure were able to overcome status differences. They worked cooperatively and in a co-inquiry mode with the consultants and hospital management in designing and developing the data-collection methods, collecting the data, making sense of the data collected, brainstorming recommendations, and preparing for feedback sessions.

The fact that by the end of the eighteen months reported here, major organizational design changes had not taken place belies the fact that tremendous change had taken place in the clarity of the issues, the quality of the discussions, and the willingness of the organization to continue learning about team care delivery. The hospital had developed a "map" of a large and messy problem (the team health care delivery process) that it was using to guide further experimentation and action.

Problems that are messy, open-ended, and/or do not fall within the purview of any one function are inherently difficult for bureaucracies to manage. Dale Zand first proposed the use of parallel learning structures specifically for this reason: the structures that are good for *performing* and solving clean, closed-ended problems are terrible for *learning* and managing open-ended problems.[5] There is a great deal to be learned from Grate Hospital about solving problems that bureaucracies cannot handle. Here we will focus mainly on two issues: (1) challenges involved in using a group problem-solving approach in bureaucratic organizations, and (2) the use of action research as the guiding inquiry process of the parallel learning structure. Other aspects of this case, particularly as they relate to team health care delivery, are available elsewhere.[6]

---

5. Zand (1974).

6. Shani & Eberhardt, 1987.

Group Problem Solving and Organization Design

The Grate Hospital case illustrates one type of parallel learning structure: a temporary structure created to solve a particular problem. In this case, the parallel learning structure was composed of three interrelated problem-solving groups—the steering committee, the study group, and the consultant team. One basic and fundamental assumption that guides parallel learning structures is the involvement of organizational members in problem solving rather than problem solving by just a few members at the top of the organization or by specialist staff groups. The use of groups for solving problems is common in OD, but represents a significant shift in managerial and organizational practices in most bureaucracies. The problem with having only senior managers do the problem solving is that they tend to have distorted views of what is going on at the bottom of the system. Subordinates often censor information as it goes up the hierarchy. This was obviously a problem at Grate, where senior managers erroneously thought that teams were functioning in an interdisciplinary fashion. In addition, senior managers are too distant from the day-to-day operations to understand the real complexities and contingencies that people face. This had also been observed at Grate in management's failure at past attempts to change clinical practices. Bureaucracy's response to this problem has been to create specialist staff groups that are charged with solving complex organizational problems. The problem with having specialist staff groups solve other people's problems is that, like senior managers, staff are most often remote from the problem, but in addition, they usually do not have the authority to implement solutions.[7] The parallel learning structure overcomes this by having those closest to the problems work on solving them, while simultaneously integrating different levels and work units to ease implementation.

There is rich and abundant literature on group problem solving, and we don't have much to offer about problem-solving processes per se. Here, we will focus on what we can learn from this case about developing problem-solving groups *within* bureaucratic systems.

---

7. Kilmann (1982) makes a similar point.

1. Knowing How to Work in Groups

Because it's so rarely done, it's very likely that members of the parallel learning structure will not have much skill or experience in effective group problem solving. Therefore, it's important to anticipate devoting some up-front time simply to teaching people how to work together in a group problem-solving format. At Grate, developing some of the basic skills around different group-related roles, such as rotation of minutes taking, approving minutes at the beginning of each meeting, and using an observer who provides the group with feedback at the end of the meeting, helped the groups operate more effectively. In OD, we often focus efforts on getting managers to be more participative. Just as important, however, is the need to develop effective *participants*.

The need to develop norms and procedures in the parallel learning structure that support cooperation, learning, and creative problem solving is critical for optimal parallel structure functioning. In the Grate case, we saw a real increase in the effectiveness of the parallel learning structure after the group was able to break down past barriers and resentments and develop cooperative norms.

2. Issues of Power and Status

The involvement of members from different levels of the organization who hold varied professional and organizational status in a setting where they meet as peers/learners/problem solvers is necessary for optimal group problem solving. Some form of explicit, temporary power equalization is required. This can be accomplished through such mechanisms as the use of consensus for all group decisions and rotating leadership of the group.

At Grate, as in many other bureaucracies, power equalization did not fit or sit well with the health care culture. In health care, top administrative support does not automatically result in physician support. Establishing physicians' commitment and support for group problem solving in which others temporarily had equal power with them was a major obstacle to overcome. As we saw in the case, many of the physicians were not only unwilling to share power but fought the notion on every front. Once the physician in the study group agreed that some of the problems might stem from physicians' behavior and showed that he was willing to let others rotate into the leadership role, the study group became much more effective. This event helped establish a new set of role relations, norms, and problem-solving style. His relinquishing of some of his authority to the group charged the group with confidence and helped establish a more equal way of working together.

Taking on senior management, through the liaison members of the study group, was another aspect of the power-equalization dynamic. In this case, we see that employees of an organization that has historically left them out of decision making need to vent their frustration about that and test senior management's willingness to be influenced by them before they will get down to any serious work. It is very important to warn managers in such organizations that this is likely to happen and that they need to respond sincerely and nondefensively when it occurs.

3. Linkage to the Formal Organization

In health care institutions authority is culturally determined via educational and professional codes and supported by legal and regulatory realities.[8] For example, the authority of the physician is almost never questioned, and physicians are reluctant to collaborate with nonphysicians. As we have seen in this chapter, the health care culture presented barriers to the initial formation of the parallel learning structure and some major challenges to its progress. The parallel structure became more legitimate over time (mostly due to its acceptance by more of the physicians) as its activities were seen to have some merit.

A critical reality of steering committees and study groups is that they live in larger systems. Because parallel learning structures, by definition, create internal cultures different from that of the formal organization, tension between the two is inevitable. Where parallel structures involve a large number of managers and employees in multiple study groups (as in Chapter 5) there tends to be a greater acceptance. In the Grate case, the study group was a "cultural island" that was not, at least initially, well linked to the formal organization. Attempts to notify organizational members about the project through internal memos had little effect. This is typical, especially in large organizations where employees have become used to new "programs" emanating from corporate offices or

---

8. Pasmore, Petee, and Bastian (1986).

senior staff that quickly fade away. Holding an organization-wide meeting to launch the parallel learning structure usually ensures that everyone has at least heard of it, but still does little to make it a reality for employees who are not directly involved.

Electing representatives to the study group by their "constituents" might, initially, increase the sense of organization-wide ownership people have for the parallel learning structure. In the long run, however, this is not an appropriate strategy. If elected, study group members become representatives of others, and this creates a debilitating dynamic that impedes groups' ability to create the informality needed for creative problem solving. There will be less likelihood of breaking through the political divisions and tensions that exist in the formal organization. A key feature of all successful applications of parallel learning structures seems to be that within the groups they overcome intergroup conflicts that are endemic to the organization.

It is when the parallel learning structure begins collecting organization-wide data that people begin to take notice. The culture of the organization will likely determine how people respond: passively, curiously, or in alarm. In our experience—and Grate exemplifies this—the most typical reaction is fear. People are afraid that information will be used against them or that they will lose something. At this point, meetings need to be held with all employees to explain what data are being collected, why, and how the information will be used.

As we saw at Grate, fear is just as likely to exist among the senior managers who launched the project as with the employees. In the Grate case, the consultants didn't do as good a job as they might have in preparing senior management for dealing with its own fears. In the early stages of setting up a parallel structure it is very important to confront senior management with the inevitable: that they will be called on to change their behavior just as much as others, and that their reaction to this will be a barometer of how successful the project will ultimately be. Keeping senior management as involved in the parallel structure as possible, either through direct membership or weekly updates, is very helpful in overcoming their inevitable resistance to change.

One of our major learnings from the Grate Hospital case came out of observing how the physicians came to give the project legitimacy. Three things seemed to be key in this. One was the experience of the two physicians in the parallel structure. Through receiving training in group dynamics and participating in a collaborative, problem-solving mode, these doctors came to appreciate that there were better ways to run clinical teams, and that all the physicians had something to learn about effective team work. Through their informal influence, other physicians began to take the project more seriously. A turning point was the lengthy questionnaire. The quality of the questionnaire, especially its completeness in assessing team dynamics, added a new level of legitimacy to the study. One section of the questionnaire, which asked people to rate 28 team leader characteristics, was, apparently, an education in itself for the doctors who filled it out. They realized that there was a lot about leading teams that they had never considered. And *all* the physicians voluntarily filled out the questionnaire.

Finally, the emphasis the consultants placed on scientific experimentation provided a link between the clinical value of experimentation and the organizational need to experiment with new ways of organizing. Finding ways to build on the existing culture is a very useful strategy in legitimizing and integrating the parallel learning structure into the formal organization. Emphasizing the value of experimental inquiry provided a point of congruence between the physicians' cultural values and the parallel structure's activities.

Action Research as a Guiding Inquiry Process

Action research was described almost four decades ago by Lewin[9] and Collier[10] as a strategy for studying and simultaneously changing systems. Lewin advocated a scientific process that included a spiral of steps, each of which is composed of planning, action, and monitoring the results of the action. The pioneering work by Lewin set the foundation for subsequent social scientists who have turned action research into a well-developed social science method of inquiry.[11]

---

9.   Lewin (1946).

10.   Collier (1946).

11.   For good, recent reviews and extensions of action research, see Susman and Evered (1978), Pasmore and Friedlander (1982), Peters and Robinson (1984), Shani and Pasmore (1985), Shani and Bushe (1987), and Reason (1988). Schein's (1987) enunciation of the elements of clinical inquiry in organizations is also in this tradition and worthwhile reading for scholars.

One of the major differences between action research and traditional research is that in action research organizational members are fully involved in the research process and share the responsibility for the effort. In an action-research process, organizational members are involved in the following activities, in roughly this order:

1. Identifying organizational issues/problem areas
2. Identifying the issues to be studied
3. Identifying what kind of information to collect
4. Deciding on the methods to be used in the effort
5. Constructing a shared understanding of the collected data
6. Exploring and experimenting with alternative solutions to the problems
7. Formulating recommendations for change
8. Formulating ways of implementing those recommendations
9. Monitoring and correcting implementation

Parallel learning structure design coupled with an action-research orientation involves at its most basic level unlocking data that are trapped in the minds of organizational members but don't, for a variety of reasons, get expressed or heard. The data get turned into usable information when shared understandings of them are developed among organizational members. The parallel learning structure provides a time and space where that process of translation and "meaning making" can take place. In the case of Grate Hospital, a process model of health care team delivery effectiveness emerged out of the collective attempt by the parallel structure members to construct a shared meaning from the interviews, surveys, and observation data.

The management of the action-research project requires the management of four key processes: the emerging socio-task system, the co-inquiry process, the integration process, and the experimentation process.[12]

---

12. Shani and Bushe (1987).

The Emerging Socio-Task System. As the parallel learning structure begins its work, the nature of the social and task relations are ambiguous. Roles, norms, and procedures are unclear. Each group goes through the typical stages of group formation and development. If the group is a collection of members from different groups and levels in the system, they are likely to bring the tensions and strains of the organization into the group. In its early stages, the behavior of the group will probably be better understood from an intergroup relations perspective.[13] For example, individuals are more likely to treat each other as representatives of their respective work units or levels, rather than as individual human beings. If there is a lot of stereotyping in the organization, members are likely to attribute these stereotypical qualities to each other. Initial interactions between members are actually interactions between group prejudices. In a very fragmented structure, there is not much organizational learning that can occur until the distortions and prejudices that keep groups apart are reduced. It is very important, then, to deal directly with the prejudices and beliefs about each other that members bring to the parallel structure. Working through stereotypes and projections to get to the real human beings leads to a tremendous release of energy in the group. In the Grate case we saw how it was very important for members to work through their anger toward physicians and senior management before they could begin to function as a group. Furthermore, we have seen and heard others talk of how major changes in a microcosm, like a parallel learning structure, coincide with similar, but unexplainable, changes in the whole system.

What is most critical in all this is the quality of the relationships that develop among all members of the parallel structure. It is through the development of high-quality relationships that information that hasn't been flowing in the past starts flowing in the groups. The quality of relationships must support the basic trust and freedom for creative problem solving and co-inquiry to flourish.

The Co-Inquiry Process The co-inquiry process refers to that state of affairs in which each of the participants, including consultants, are defined as co-learners. This requires emphasis on

---

13. Alderfer (1987), Taylor and Moghaddam (1987). See also Chapter 5.

joint determination of issue definition, data collection, analysis, and interpretation. It will not always be possible for everyone to be involved in all decisions, especially when the parallel structure is first being formed. It is, however, important to define everyone as *learners* and to hold off the inevitable pressures for performance. It is also not useful to pretend that specialized expertise does not exist, but this is more a question of timing. In the early stages of group formation, it is more important to have the groups develop a sense of their own identity and power. This may require supporting the fiction that everyone is equal. Once the groups are functioning effectively, it is no big deal to defer to some other person or group's greater expertise on a particular subject.

In the early stages of parallel structure formation, those with differentiated roles, like consultant or facilitator, will be the target of group dependence. This gives the consultant some useful early influence for modeling appropriate behavior. It is more effective to give direction in the form of a problem-solving facilitator than as a task expert so that the groups don't become incapable of functioning on their own. The aim of the consultant should be to provide the minimum necessary leadership to get the groups functioning and to encourage the emergence of leadership from within the group. It seems most effective for the consultant to work toward a position of having little to do with the content of each group and focus on maintaining healthy group process. Moreover, a consultant should be spending most of his or her time managing the boundaries of the parallel structure, not the groups themselves.

Part of the facilitation of co-inquiry requires a respect for the nature of "tacit knowledge"[14] and an ability to aid people in articulating what they "know but cannot say." This requires developing group norms that respect and encourage the expression of intuitive glimpses, half-thoughts, and fuzzy ideas. A related aspect is helping people say what they know but are afraid to say. In either case, co-inquiry is dampened by large power differentials and large status gaps between members, which generally tend to reduce trust. There must be allowance for the expression of potentially conflict-producing ideas. This is one reason why learning isn't taking place in the formal organization, so steps must be taken to empower the

---

14.   Polanyi (1966).

disenfranchised within the parallel structure. The use of consensus decision making and rotating group leadership are the minimum necessary conditions.

The Integration Process. The integration process refers to the collective attempt to construct shared meaning out of the data. The parallel structure brings together individuals with different personal objectives, methods of inquiry, perceptions, and frames of reference. Working toward the integration of this diversity is the most powerful force for creativity and the emergence of new ideas. It requires suspending preconceived and well-indoctrinated categories and beliefs. Everything must be up for question and possible disconfirmation. This can't be done without a well-functioning group. Hopefully, having worked through issues definition and data-collection methods, the groups will be fully functional by the time they have data to interpret.

In cases where shared meaning cannot be arrived at, integration is aided by a commitment to implementing recommendations on an experimental basis. By not having to be committed to a particular interpretation of the data before action is taken, people can move forward, try something out, and see if it works. In this way, arguments over interpretation of the data (i.e., the integration process) can be grounded in actual outcomes.

The Experimentation Process. The entire parallel learning structure intervention can be viewed—and often is viewed by organizational members—as experimental. All decisions, commitments, and outcomes are open to modification based on trial-and-error learning. Experimentation is a core value of action research and of the parallel structure. By joining the parallel structure, employees and managers become involved in an experiment of new ways of relating at work. Throughout the action-research cycle various ways of defining problems, collecting data, and analyzing results are open to change based on experience and analysis. Further, experimentation and data become the accepted procedure for resolving disagreements (rather than power, status, or verbal skills). Managing the experimentation process primarily involves creating space in the organization for experiments to take place without people becoming identified with their success or failure.

Key Points in Using Parallel Learning Structures to Solve Problems Bureaucracies Cannot Handle

1. Recognize that the purpose of the parallel learning structure is to learn, not perform, and that it will take time for people in an organization oriented to performance to get comfortable with that.

2. The parallel structure is created to work on a specific problem or set of problems. It is important to spend a lot of up-front time defining the problem (staying "problem-minded") before moving toward problem solution.

3. The steering committee should be made up of the senior members with the clout to implement wide-ranging changes as a result of the parallel structure's recommendations, but should also include representatives of different points of view.

4. Senior managers should be warned that groups will test their ability to influence them early in the process, and this is likely to be expressed in a resentful manner. They must also be warned that they will become uncomfortable when the parallel structure begins to look at senior management's role in "the problem," and that they must show openness to change.

5. Membership in parallel learning structure groups should not be imposed on people, and composition should reflect the different constituencies affected by the problems under consideration. Liaison members between the steering committee and each study group are very important.

6. To launch the parallel structure, it is very useful to have a meeting away from the workplace where the scope of the problem(s) to be dealt with is extensively discussed and the operating philosophy of the parallel learning structure is affirmed.

7. Groups will need training in group problem solving and decision making. Interventions may be required to create the conditions for optimal group effectiveness. Parallel structure groups should use an action-research method

for approaching their problems and may require some training in that as well.

8. A key issue will be linkage between the parallel learning structure and the rest of the organization. The cultural differences in operating style between the parallel learning structure and the formal organization need to be explained and accepted.

4

Implementing
System-Transforming
Innovations

Most organizational innovations help to enhance or improve some aspect of the business without changing the overall nature of the organization itself. We call these "system-maintaining" innovations. Other innovations, however, when fully implemented, affect fundamental aspects of the organization, creating a need to change many segments of the organization. Introducing computers into a business that has not used them in the past is one example. Many of the "world-class" manufacturing techniques—such as "just-in-time" materials handling and total quality control—also have this "transforming" quality when implemented in American factories. System-transforming innovations are those that push up against the political, technical, and/or cultural systems in an organization, creating change in the very nature of the organization itself. This is similar to the distinction between first- and second-order change.[1] A first-order change has some magnitude, but a second-order change changes the system itself. As a result, system-transforming innovations are the most difficult innovations to implement successfully.

Portions of this chapter are reprinted by permission from Bushe, "Use of a Parallel Learning Structure to Implement System Transforming Innovations: The Case of Statistical Process Control," *The Journal of Managerial Psychology,* Vol. 4, No. 4, 1989.

1. Watzlawick, Weakland, and Fisch (1974).

Case: Triburg Manufacturing

Larry Stern slammed his phone down with a bang. "Those idiots think that charts on a wall mean our processes are under control," he said out loud to the room filled with mildly amused and sympathetic SPC coordinators. Such frustrations were becoming a daily routine for the group of statistical process control (SPC) coordinators at Triburg Manufacturing. A few short months ago, this group had been created in a fanfare of high hopes and excitement. Six of the best young supervisors had been hand-picked to receive hundreds of hours of training to become the vanguard for the implementation of SPC throughout the plant. Now a deep pessimism pervaded the group.

The Innovation

Statistical process control (SPC) or statistical quality control (SQC) are two names for a method of controlling manufacturing processes to ensure that outputs conform to specifications. Developed in the 1940s and '50s, this technique was largely ignored in North America. Japan, however, launched a national program to implement the use of SPC, and the Japanese attribute much of their success in world markets to its use. To appreciate SPC fully, it is useful to contrast it with traditional, North American methods of quality control.

In North America, because of an assumed conflict of goals, quality control has traditionally been regarded as a function separate from manufacturing. Manufacturing's goal is to maximize output and minimize cost; quality control's goal is to ensure that only those outputs that meet specifications are shipped. Typically, a quality inspector goes through manufactured goods just prior to shipment and separates the good from the bad. Such "ship" or "don't ship" information is referred to in SPC as "attribute data." It generally provides little information that is useful in understanding the causes of defects and spots these defects only after productive resources have been spent manufacturing the product. This "end-of-the-line" type of quality control inspection is one of the reasons that hidden plant costs or rework costs in North America have been so high.

With SPC, however, an attempt is made to understand all the variables that affect output and how they vary together. In particular, statistical methods are used to detect special causes of variation and to understand what limits of variation will produce defects. First, the process capability of a manufacturing process must be known. This is the variation that will always be present and the best the process is capable of producing in its current state. Then, tolerances for each critical variable to ensure that the final product meets specifications must be known. Finally, operators sample parts as they move through the manufacturing process to ensure that they fall within these tolerances. As a result, one can be assured that the final output is within specification to whatever level the process is capable of attaining. In SPC, quality control is a line-management and operator function, and variable data are collected that aid in pinpointing the causes of defects. In one study, Japanese manufacturers using SPC had field failure rates 15 to 70 times lower than their U. S. competitors.[2]

On the surface, SPC appears to fit into the traditional "control mentality" of manufacturing management. In reality, SPC contravenes many of the usual political and cultural norms of American manufacturing.[3] Some examples are its emphasis on managing multivariable relations, using data collected by workers to make decisions, preventive maintenance versus the "don't-fix-it-unless-it's-broke" manufacturing norm, and giving workers authority to stop production processes when they are out of control.

Background to the Intervention

Triburg Manufacturing first became interested in SPC in 1980, when a young quality supervisor, Tim, who had shown keen interest in Japanese manufacturing methods had a serendipitous opportunity to have a series of informal conversations with the plant manager. He was put on special assignment to study what the Japanese were doing. He and the plant manager became convinced that SPC was one of the innovations they should adopt. During this time, Larry Stern, another young quality supervisor, also became convinced of SPC's importance and, together with Tim, began trying to implement it in the plant.

The first problem they ran into was indifference. Manufacturing managers had many problems and competing demands and SPC seemed like a less than optimal use of their time. Finally, in the

---

2. Garvin (1983)

3. See Bushe (1985) and Bushe (1988b).

summer of 1981, they convinced one department head to try out a project on a new paint system that had wild fluctuation in yields. Given that an average of 45 percent of items painted were being scrapped, and the department head had no idea what to do about it, the SPC project was a last-ditch effort with little to lose. Tim and Larry convinced the supervisor and workers in the area to help collect precise data on each day's production. Many months went into this effort with little to show. They discovered that they really did not know what the variables in the paint system were, and neither did the manufacturer of the system!

The first few weeks of data collection proved to be erroneous because first shift had failed to inform second shift of what they were doing. Then, when they thought they had proved that the problem was in the design of the system, the engineers refused to believe the data. They had to spend another three weeks redoing their experiments and collecting more data before the department head would act. As it turned out, changing the system increased yield somewhat, but only a little. It was five months before they finally nailed the problem—variances in the paint itself that had been tolerated by their old paint system were messing up the new system. Since paint was bought by divisional purchasers, the plant then had to spend a lot more time convincing the purchasing department to add new specifications to paint purchase. While waiting for something to happen with the paint, the supervisors and workers in the area became disenchanted with the lack of action and stopped collecting the data. When the new paint finally arrived, the whole data-collection process had to be started up again to ensure that they now had the paint process under control. Full implementation of SPC requires ongoing data collection and monitoring so that new variances can be identified and corrected quickly. It was impossible, however, to keep people motivated to collect the data after the paint problem appeared to be solved but no visible action had been taken.

Still trying to convince more senior managers and department heads about the importance of SPC, Tim and Larry circumvented formal channels and invited a manufacturing Vice-President from another division of the company to come and give a talk to plant management. This VP's talk went over extremely well, and senior management decided to start using SPC more. Larry Stern was made a full-time "SPC coordinator." Tim was already on a loosely defined "special assignment," and implementation of SPC became one of his responsibilities. At the beginning of 1982, a committee of senior managers was created to assign SPC projects to each manufacturing department and meet weekly with each department head to review progress. Each department, in turn, created a task force that was supposed to work on the project. All members of these task forces received ten hours of training in SPC. Over the next few months, various problems stymied most of these efforts. In one department, the project team got into a major fight with plant engineering over the validity of the findings, and the team disbanded in disgust. In another department, it became apparent only after three months that data were being collected improperly. It was not clear whether this was willful or not, but concerns were surfaced that SPC data would target who "isn't doing their job" and be used to punish people. In two other departments, managers were loath to assign people to the SPC projects, most likely because the departments were over their labor budgets and needed to keep people focused on production. All projects were adversely affected by a major plant layoff and the subsequent movement and "bumping" of workers out of the areas where they were involved in SPC projects. And most people who had received SPC training had forgotten it by the time they were actually working on a project.

A recognition of the need for more trained project leaders and eventual training of all plant personnel coincided with an opportunity to receive state funding for industrial renewal. Tim and Larry put together a proposal to get state funding to pay for two years of salary and the training of six SPC coordinators. By summer it became clear that they would get this funding and more money to pay for training all plant personnel in SPC.

In the summer of 1982, a special meeting of senior managers and department heads was called to discuss the lack of action with SPC. The original committee structure had collapsed from lack of use (little to report, meetings often canceled to deal with some "crisis"). At this meeting lots of blaming and finger-pointing occurred. The usual fighting between service and manufacturing managers threatened to get out of hand, though a new openness about the issues was also evident. The problem of staffing these projects got aired, though nothing was done because they expected the new SPC coordinators to alleviate the problem. It also became evident to Tim and Larry that many of the managers still didn't really understand what SPC was or what its potential was. To overcome this problem, they arranged for senior managers to visit another company in the area that was more advanced in its use of SPC.

Once more project teams were created. In almost all cases, an initial burst of enthusiasm sputtered out as the groups ran into problems of group formation, authority relations, and being overwhelmed by the task in front of them. Used to an authoritarian style of management, the groups didn't know how to operate as a group of peers learning together. Furthermore, neither they nor their management had defined their task as learning; they were operating under pressure to perform. Without an individual in the group championing the process, they floundered. In the few cases where they were able to get data collected and problems pinpointed, they then ran into problems getting the necessary resources to fix the problems. Sometimes they needed engineering help, and other times they needed material resources. There was no system for responding to their requests other than the conventional upward reporting through the hierarchy. Sometimes requests for resources weren't passed on by department heads who had other priorities. Requests for help from overworked engineers and skilled tradesmen fell on deaf ears. Some problems that other plants had experienced with union resistance to workers' collecting data (e.g., "that's a quality technician's job") didn't materialize at Triburg, probably because it already had an active quality of work life (QWL) process with many quality circles operating. In many cases, quality circles were eager to learn and use SPC techniques, but the resources to train them were not available.

Creation of SPC Coordinators

Tim and Larry realized at this point that implementing SPC was not just a technical problem. Social and organizational issues seemed to be much more difficult to manage. In selecting the SPC coordinators, they ensured that good interpersonal skills, along with technical know-how, were selection criteria and that the coordinators would get OD training as well as statistical training.

In August, five SPC coordinators were selected from among first-level supervisors in the plant to join Larry. Tim continued to have broader responsibilities. The position was a lateral transfer, not a promotion, and the assignment was only for two years. For the first month they were trained in SPC by an outside consultant. They became zealous advocates; they were out to save the plant. Unleashed upon their respective departments, they ran into the machine bureaucracy. They found it difficult to get the attention of busy managers, who had multiple responsibilities and who barely understood what they were talking about. They faced an uncertain future. State funding would last for two years, but then what? A decision was made at senior levels *not* to make SPC a job element of supervisors. Thus, it appeared that the formal organization was not backing them up.

At Tim's suggestion the coordinators initiated a process for defining their roles. They began with the senior production and engineering managers, and obtained an agreement that their role was *not* simply to do statistical analysis, but to facilitate the adoption of SPC in the line organization. Next, they went on to discuss their roles with department heads. Here the main mode of facilitation envisioned was training. They were expected to train managers and operators in SPC. After the role negotiations were completed, the production manager asked them to develop a two-year plan for having 100 percent of the plant using SPC. To comply, they developed a document that time-lined a sequence of training activities.

By mid-October 1982, morale among the coordinators was very low. The fact that the office and computer terminals promised them had yet to appear exacerbated the situation, but more important was a deep sense of frustration. Intuitively, they knew that the role-negotiation process and the two-year plan were just smoke and mirrors. They knew that training alone would not change things, that there were culturally ingrained habits that also had to change. Their boss was holding them to their plan, which reinforced their perception that nobody understood, nobody cared, and all of this was just more window dressing. They believed themselves to be victims of the very processes they were trying to change. They did not see their boss as holding them to *their own* plans. What they saw was an unthinking subservience to making "the numbers look right." Their disillusionment was reinforced by corporate requests to report how many SPC charts were being kept on the floor. Around them decisions were being made based on hunches and opinions, not data and analysis. Furthermore, they perceived themselves as being lowly first-line supervisors, in staff positions, with no authority to do anything. Even though they reported to the production manager ("the number-two man"), they did not perceive this as a power base. Rather, they feared him, and saw him as cold, impersonal, manipulating, uncaring, narrow, and intractable. In the presence of this manager, these six bright, articulate, and aggressive young men would become sullen, passive, and nonresponsive. They would apparently listen to what he said, then later try to "interpret" what he had meant. In retrospect, they agreed that they had projected all their negative fantasies about the organization onto this one man.

When the training in OD began in December 1982, the coordinators were confused, angry, and worried that they had been set up to fail. The training program consisted of three-day workshops each month for six months, and included problem-solving and strategy sessions as well as educational content.[4] During the first three-day class, the group targeted their poor relationship with their boss (the production manager) as their most critical problem. During the class, they devised a plan for co-opting the department heads and using them as a power base to influence the production manager and develop a "realistic" implementation plan. That they did not initiate this strategy for two more months attests to the degree of fear they were experiencing and the amount of courage it took to pull it off. As 1982 came to an end, the SPC coordinators were attempting to have a job description written up, which included their key job elements. This action was clearly motivated by despair that nothing would happen with SPC and that they would be blamed. At least with clearly stated job elements, each could make sure to do those. The team was fragmenting, and each coordinator was following his own conscience in respect to how he intervened in his department. Their approaches ranged from those still trying to nudge others into using statistics to those doing all the department's SPC work themselves. There was a pervasive sense of lack of support, and there were numerous events that could be pointed to justify that feeling.

Creation of the Parallel Structure

In January 1983, the coordinators put their plan into action. They convened a meeting with the heads of manufacturing departments.

---

4. At first the SPC coordinators were leery of this "behavioral science crap," as they called it, and if this training program had been given to them just as they were hired, they probably would have learned very little. Having found themselves running into walls for four months, they were much more prepared to learn. The fact that, a year later, all of them considered this course the most important and useful one of the dozen or so they had taken reinforces the assumption that social dynamics are at the root of implementation difficulties.

Using group problem-solving procedures they had learned in class, criteria for developing a realistic implementation plan were developed, along with a lot of common understanding. To their surprise, the department heads were not angry at them (lowly staff people) for convening a meeting. In fact, the meeting went very well, and was followed by a second one convened to develop a plan that centered on using a parallel learning structure to guide implementation. They envisioned something similar to the task-force structure they had used before, but with broader-based membership and a learning- (as opposed to performing-) oriented mandate. The steering committee's role would be less "monitoring and evaluating" and "more facilitating and enabling."

A week later, the coordinators convened a meeting with the heads of service departments. During this meeting they developed a similar plan. A week later, they brought both groups together to work out the slight differences in the two plans. Unifying the plan was not only a logical necessity, but also satisfied the need to build bridges between the manufacturing and service departments. This meeting went extremely well, which was notable because it was unusual for service and manufacturing heads to meet without fighting.

This group of department heads and coordinators then "demanded" a meeting with senior management. At that meeting, a revolt-like atmosphere developed, and one of the department heads, while pounding his fist on the table, told the production manager "how it's going to be." The senior managers agreed to the plan. The SPC coordinators were euphoric. They had developed a solid power base with the department heads. They now had a "realistic plan," and they now had some credibility for having pulled off this series of meetings. Soon after, the production manager commented that the most impressive thing about the meeting was the air of cooperation between service and manufacturing. After this, the problems between the SPC coordinators and their boss rapidly faded as the coordinators took initiative in speaking up. Ironically, they came to discover that the production manager was a kind and gentle man whose apparent coldness was actually shyness. After this "revolt" the SPC coordinators had very little trouble working easily at all levels of the organization, and they came to be seen by senior managers and department heads as resources not only in SPC, but also in the areas of group process and problem solving.

The plan was as follows. A parallel learning structure steering committee was set up consisting of the production manager and the three senior managers responsible for servicing production (engineering, materials and quality). Manufacturing departments could propose SPC projects to this committee for consideration. If the steering committee "bought" the project, it was also making a commitment to provide adequate resources for the project and to step in to remove any barriers the project might encounter. (The steering committee and department heads also made an agreement to stop "fire fighting" and do whatever was necessary to use data and analysis rather than hunches and opinions to solve production problems.) Once a project was approved, a project team was created that included representatives from each service department as well as the supervisor and some workers in the area affected. Teams typically had some assigned members and others who had volunteered. Team leaders were not appointed. One or two SPC coordinators were also team members. Ostensibly there to provide consultation and training in SPC *and* group dynamics, their greater expertise led them to emerge as informal leaders in most teams. Within the first month, there was a project team functioning in each of the five manufacturing departments.

Concurrent SPC Coordinator Activities

The plan also included SPC training for all managers and a large percentage of the work force. The production manager asked the SPC coordinators to develop and deliver the training program. The coordinators balked at this, fearing their lack of experience and credibility. They argued for buying outside contractors using the state funds. The production manager was adamant, so in conjunction with their OD training course, they developed a ten-hour program that had five hours of SPC and five hours of group problem solving. As it turned out, the training program was a big hit in the plant, and this further bolstered the credibility and confidence of the coordinators. After a few months, however, they discovered that if the people who took the class were not involved in an SPC project, they quickly forgot the material. They came to appreciate that training was most effective when done within the parallel structure groups on an as-needed basis. Instead of randomly training everyone in the plant, they would give the ten-hour class to a newly formed project team, intact. This not only conveyed the material, but provided a team-building opportunity for the project team. By this point, the OD training was over and the consultants phased out. They had worked extensively with the SPC coordinators and Tim in a shadow consulting capacity, but had not ever been a part of the parallel learning structure.

As the coordinators worked with more and more people, they discovered that few managers had any imagination when it came to the possibilities of SPC. People's understanding of SPC was usually limited to what they had personally been involved with or had seen. For example, after the first year of parallel structure operation, a large minority of managers thought SPC meant inspecting scrapped parts to get accurate defect information, even though all of them had taken the SPC training. As it turned out, the way most people learned what SPC really could be was by becoming involved in a coordinator-driven project. This created a dilemma for the coordinators, who saw their job as teaching and enabling others rather than doing the SPC work themselves. In each situation, they had to assess how much to lead and show people what they didn't know, and how much to hang back and let people develop ownership of the process.

Simultaneous Inquiry and Action

The parallel learning structure, and the fact that department heads felt ownership for it, helped to resolve many of the problems experienced in earlier implementation efforts. Because service managers were involved in collecting and analyzing SPC data, they didn't resist the findings. Things no longer "fell through the cracks." Parallel structure members felt that it was okay to circumvent the normal chain of command and deal directly with anyone in the organization. Findings from SPC projects were *acted on*. Supervisors discovered they could draw more attention to a problem if they "SPC'ed it," thus increasing their motivation to use it. Providing training and facilitation in group dynamics helped people work in the groups effectively. The parallel structure also provided a forum where major issues, such as the fear that SPC would be used to punish people, could be addressed and managed.

One very big issue was that in the past managers had normally "fudged" their production and quality figures to "hit the numbers" in their public reports. SPC, however, required complete and accurate reporting. Once SPC data were collected on a manufacturing process, it would look as though the managers had been lying in the past. It was very difficult for any manager to voice this concern, but the SPC coordinators got wind of it and brought it to the steering committee's attention. The steering committee issued a statement acknowledging that "hitting the numbers" had been the name of the game in the past, that the ground rules were now changing, and that nobody would be held accountable for having played under different rules in the past. This allayed most managers' fears.

Problems of resistance, turf, and indifference still got in the way, but a momentum was established and a parallel structure existed through which many of the problems could get resolved. By summer 1983, Triburg Manufacturing's success at solving its problems began to get corporate attention. New work came in the door and, partly through the use of SPC, the plant was able to take it on successfully. In addition, the corporation was requiring all managers to attend special training in total quality management. Apparently, the corporate personnel who offered the training program at the plant were impressed with the sophistication of the change process there. Triburg volunteered to pilot the Quality Management Program (QMP) and was accepted. A manufacturing department head was put on special assignment as director of QMP (interestingly, this was the department head who had the first successful SPC project in 1981).

Other good things happened. For example, Triburg became the first supplier to be removed from a customer's "quality inspection list," due to consistently high quality. From all reports, management meetings were more productive and less stressful. There was more planning and rational decision making. Problems were being solved and staying solved. Department heads were developing good, cooperative working relationships with each other. The SPC steering committee met regularly and ensured that resources were allocated to tackle major projects. Corporate-wide meetings of SPC coordinators from different plants began at this time, and it quickly became evident that Triburg was far ahead of the other plants in implementation. Hourly workers were involved with SPC in every department and a number of them had come up with some very impressive solutions to problems. During a corporate executive tour in September, nearly all the presentations were made by hourly employees or first-line supervisors and involved SPC projects. In October, the plant reported approximately one million dollars in annual savings from eleven SPC projects.

Analysis and Some Learnings from the Case

Statistical process control is a system-transforming innovation in most American manufacturing plants. Even in the Triburg case, the plant has only begun to use it and has yet to fully institutionalize its use. To do so would require changes in factory reporting and control systems, worker authority, the nature of supervision, the role of quality and purchasing (to name only two functions), and the very way managers think about manufacturing. Here we're going to focus less on SPC per se, and more on the parallel learning structure's utility for implementing system-transforming innovations.

What Is a System-Transforming Innovation?

To begin to understand this concept, you need to understand the difference between primary and secondary attributes of innovations.[5] A primary attribute is something inherent in the innovation. A secondary attribute is something that is true of the innovation only because of the context within which it is implemented. For example, the price of a new machine is a primary attribute; its price will be the same (generally speaking) no matter who buys it. Its "cost," however, is a secondary attribute, because what is costly for one firm can be relatively cheap for another.

"System-transforming" is a secondary attribute of an innovation.[6] The first time a computer system is implemented in a company, it affects the basic organization of that company. Later, when a new computer system is implemented, it will probably be simply a "system-maintaining" innovation. System-transforming innovations (STIs) are those that affect several social and technical subsystems and directly affect relations among a large percentage of people in the organization in which they are implemented. By contrast, system-maintaining innovations (SMIs) affect only the subsystems in which they are implemented and fit easily into the existing pattern of relationships among people.

As a few subsystems in an organization are changed to accommodate the STI, they create the need for change in ever more

---

5. Downs and Mohr (1976).

6. After Bushe developed this concept, we discovered that a few others have begun making a similar distinction: Ettlie, Bridges and O'Keefe (1984), Cohn and Turyn (1984), Nord and Tucker (1987).

subsystems. One of the characteristics of STIs is that it is virtually impossible to know, at the outset, what all the implications of the innovation will be. The rippling effect, like small waves generated in a container, can build up into turbulent water and sink the innovation before some calm is restored. People in departments far from the "epicenter" of the STI will either have to shift to accommodate to it or be the wall against which the innovation founders. When Triburg began implementing SPC, it had no idea that a major impediment to full institutionalization would be the accounting and control system used by the corporation.[7] They didn't know how to even begin to address this problem.

Strategies for Implementation

Strategies that are very useful for implementing SMIs don't seem to work well with STIs; in fact, some can backfire. For example, one useful strategy for implementing an SMI is to pilot it first in one area, work the bugs out, show others the advantages of the innovation, and then diffuse it. Pilot-diffusion strategies for STIs not only don't work, they generate even greater resistance to the innovation. This was painfully learned (over and over again) in quality-of-worklife and socio-technical systems projects throughout the seventies and eighties. The pilot area could show fantastic results, but the innovation would not diffuse. A similar thing seemed to happen with the paint-room project at Triburg. It was as though people saw that implementing the STI would require so much change in their own work behavior that they would search for reasons why the innovation wouldn't work in their own organization or department. And the piloting process gave them time to put up the barricades and make sure they could avoid it. One of the advantages of the parallel learning structure strategy is that it is a system-wide implementation process from the start. As such, it gives the forces of resistance less time to coalesce and harden.

Three Moments in Implementation

We have found it useful to think about three "moments" in the process by which a person adopts a new way of doing things. We label these "know how?", "can get?", and "want to?". By asking these

---

7. For more on this, see Bushe (1985).

questions we find out what the organization can do to facilitate adoption of innovations.

1. Know How?

First we ask the question, does this person *know how* to do what we're asking him or her to do? This is fairly obvious to most managers, and companies usually do provide time and money to train people in new techniques and other innovations. But as the Triburg case showed, if your only implementation strategy is training, then your attempt is doomed to failure. First, training doesn't begin to address the complex ripple effects an STI creates. Second, if the training isn't immediately used, it tends to be forgotten. One of the advantages of using a parallel learning structure for implementing STIs is that training resources can be focused on precisely those people and groups who need them on an as-needed basis. This "just-in-time" training appears to lock in the know-how in a way classroom formats just can't match.

2. Can Get?

The second question we ask is *can they get* what they need to use the innovation? Initially, Triburg ran into all sorts of "can-get" problems in its implementation effort. Groups couldn't get engineers to believe the data; they couldn't get service departments to fix machines that weren't obviously broken; managers couldn't get divisional purchasing to change their purchase specifications. Motivation to adopt an innovation wanes quickly if people can't get what they need to use it. The parallel learning structure is of tremendous use in addressing "can-get" issues.

Most "can-get" issues arise out of poor organizational integration, and this is a problem endemic to bureaucracies. In the Triburg case, we saw problems arising from poor integration between functions, departments, levels of hierarchy, and shifts and between the plant and corporate offices. Because STIs, by definition, require change in the work behavior of people in so many different groups, there will always be these sorts of "can-get" problems. To the extent that the parallel learning structure brings people from each of these groups together, it promotes integration around the innovation itself.

3. Want To?

The third "moment" in adoption leads to the question, does the person *want to* use the innovation? There are many issues concerning motivation too numerous to mention here. Obviously, "know how" and "can get" affect motivation tremendously. We expect that an innovation that makes people's jobs better will generate its own motivation, but we can't always foresee what all the "want-to" issues might be. At Triburg, for example, no one anticipated the fear that SPC data would be used to highlight and punish past inaccuracies in reporting. A major advantage of the parallel learning structure is that it provides a forum where these issues can be surfaced and sent to the right place for resolution. In this case, the steering committee could and did create a policy of overlooking past reporting practices.

All the problems generated by an STI cannot be known in advance. The parallel learning structure creates the time and space to continuously learn what the issues are, formulate solutions, and route them to where they need to be implemented. Without such a process, the chances of full implementation of an STI are slim. The parallel learning structure should be designed to house and enhance those processes.

Using Supervisors as Change Agents

One of the things that made the parallel learning structure work at Triburg was the existence of six full-time, internal consultants, highly trained in the STI. They functioned as a semiautonomous group with no designated supervisor, reporting to the production manager. Most STIs will require people with expertise for full implementation. Increasingly, manufacturing organizations undertaking work innovations are assigning line supervisors and managers to new, change-agent roles. They are given such titles as coordinator, facilitator, trainer, or analyst. Their job is to implement a set of techniques that have ramifications far beyond the techniques themselves. Often they find themselves reporting to someone many levels above them in the hierarchy. As we saw in the Triburg case, moving line supervisors into ambiguous staff roles reporting to senior managers is very likely to create severe distortions, projections, and authority dynamics. Those with personalities least likely to be awed and intimidated by their new boss are also unlikely to be chosen for sensitive, change-agent roles. The SPC coordinators were no exception, and a risky intervention was necessary to help the group find its center of power. Once they did, their effectiveness as change agents increased dramatically. Note, however, the many advantages they had over the more typical case where only one or two supervisors are put into such roles:

1. They had a group of six to provide some safety in numbers as well as more ideas, talents, and perspectives.
2. They had a role model and ally in Tim, who was already well connected in the plant and was an extremely sophisticated change agent.
3. They had a very large training budget and were provided training not only in the technique (SPC), but in being change agents.

One suspects that where only one person is given a change-agent role, the obstacles to implementing an STI effectively are overwhelming. The change agent trying to implement an STI in a large bureaucracy is a lot like David taking on Goliath. To be at all successful, he or she cannot pay much heed to the traditional culture, which is attuned to the status quo and operates by chain of command. Since the change agent can't be afraid to bend a few rules, he or she must feel supported and trusted by the senior manager(s) he or she reports to. The temptation to make the numbers look right and play to the boss's own perspective (which is probably limited, as the boss has had a lot less training) is enormous.

The fact that all the coordinators were on the same level as first-line supervisors created certain advantages and disadvantages. The disadvantages had mainly to do with the limitations people at the bottom of hierarchies place on themselves. In addition to the distorted authority dynamics already discussed, those at the bottom tend to view themselves as powerless and to assume the attributes of the "victim." The advantage was that the position is nonthreatening to just about everyone else in the organization. If the change agents were, hierarchically, on the same level as department heads or senior managers, they would be subject to the same distortions of information that anyone at the top of a system is. They would have much less access to the true feelings and opinions of workers and supervisors. On the other hand, the same distortions tend not to occur in a downward flow. Senior managers are much less threatened by discussing things with someone who is, hierarchically, much further down. It's as though when people in hierarchies look up, they see the position; when they look down, they see the person. Having change agents placed near the bottom provides them with enormous access to the whole organization if they can find a way to overcome the natural tendency to feel trapped at the bottom and unwittingly place self-imposed limits on their activities.

Within Triburg, virtually everyone agreed that the coordinators' role was to facilitate the use of SPC, not to do the statistical work of the plant. With any STI, a large part of the experts' job is to transfer their knowledge to others and, essentially, work themselves out of a job. In theory this makes sense, but in practice there is a dilemma. Even by the end of 1983, many managers at Triburg did not really understand SPC or what it could do for them. Each one thought he or she knew what it was. This was mainly because a lot of areas had, at some point, gone through a process of analyzing scrap; that is, counting up the different defects and charting them and discovering what their various percentages were. This is a first step in using SPC, but for a significant number of supervisors, this was all SPC was. Having taken the ten-hour training course didn't make much difference. Not surprisingly, these supervisors showed little interest in using SPC unless there was a particular quality problem to be solved. They did not appear resistant to SPC, they simply didn't understand what process control really meant.

The dilemma for change agents is that their direct involvement in a parallel learning structure group—doing the statistical work, deciding what data to collect, setting up the data-collection system, and doing the analyses—appeared to be the only way supervisors and workers developed an appreciation of what SPC could do. On the one hand, if the change agents are the only ones who actually apply the STI, we can expect that many managers will be quite happy to leave it all up to them, hindering the institutionalization of the change. On the other hand, if the change agents don't get personally involved in using the STI, people don't get an opportunity to learn it in a hands-on manner. Finding the fine line between these two positions is a difficult and delicate matter.

To summarize, moving lower-level supervisors into change-agent roles has advantages and disadvantages. It appears that the disadvantages can be overcome if the change agent(s) can break out of hierarchically embedded roles. One of the most often described ways of doing this in the T-group and OD literature, and the one that occurred at Triburg, is to go through an act of rebelliousness "successfully." In working to institutionalize a system-transforming innovation, change agents must remain sensitive to when people don't really understand the innovation, but say they do. A dilemma change agents face is in maintaining a clear separation between their roles as teachers and the managers' roles as doers when teaching requires some doing.

Key Points in Using Parallel Learning Structures to Implement System-Transforming Innovations

1. Create a steering committee with the representation and clout to change significant organizational policies and procedures in response to ripples from the STI. Assume from the beginning that all of the effects of the innovation can not be known at the onset. Ensure that the committee adopts a learning (as opposed to performing) posture. In practice this means that the study groups should *not* "regularly report on their progress" to the steering committee. This sets up performance pressures. Rather, study groups should meet with the steering committee when they feel a need to do so.

2. Ensure that senior managers of departments not directly affected by the STI know what is going on and appreciate that they may be affected down the road. Where that probability exists, get them and their people involved in the parallel learning structure.

3. Form study groups in each department or area where the innovation is to be implemented. Ensure that each group has representatives of other departments/areas that are interdependent with the target department. Ensure that the groups get some training in how to function effectively as teams as well as in the STI. Stress the learning nature of their task. In the Triburg case, the innovation involved small-group problem solving, but not all STIs will. Where it doesn't, the group's task is to meet weekly to learn

about the implications of the STI as it is being implemented, surface implementation problems, and either resolve them or send them to the steering committee for resolution.

4. Have enough people with expertise in the innovation to be able to provide continuous consulting and training support to the study groups and others who must learn how to use the innovation. These consultants should also have an appreciation of organizational change processes.

5. Provide employees with brief overview training in the STI, but don't waste money on extensively training people who won't immediately use it. Seek ways to provide "just-in-time" training.

5

Developing Cooperative Labor-Management Relations

With the globalization of manufacturing competition has come the need for continuous, rapid improvement in the quality of products and the effectiveness of manufacturing organization.[1] One salient reality of most manufacturing companies in North America is that they are unionized. If relations between labor and management are hostile and distrustful, companies will probably not be able to make the sweeping changes needed on the shop floor to compete successfully in world markets. Learning to cooperate and trust one another can be a difficult task for workers and managers, especially if there is a history of deceit, broken promises, and dirty tactics. Obviously, there must be a recognition of common interests and a sincere desire on the part of key managers and union leaders to find win-win solutions to their concerns. Even with such a transformational vision in place, new structures are needed to help people learn to see each other in new ways and to cooperate where they once fought. For as much as a leader may expound a new vision of cooperation, there will be many others who have never experienced it, are not sure they want it, and/or don't believe it is possible. In these cases, a parallel

---

1. "World-class manufacturing" is now considered to include at least "just-in-time" materials handling, total quality management, and computerized integrated process. For a fascinating account of transformed manufacturing, written as a novel, see Goldratt and Cox (1986).

learning structure can be a place where union officials, managers, and workers come together to seek common interests, test the sincerity of others, and experience the possibilities of interdependence.

Case: Pittown Assembly

The Pittown plant of United Automotive, built before World War II, had 7,000 employees on two shifts. The plant operated two car-assembly lines, grossing about $500,000,000 a year in sales. Prior to the intervention to be described, relations within the plant were very poor. Local union stewards perceived their job as "getting that supervisor's goat." The President of the local union would regularly relieve his bowels in the plant manager's car to the delight of many workers (and, secretly, some managers). The plant averaged 900 open grievances a week. Relations between levels of management were also poor. Supervisors and managers tended to not trust their superiors, and there was little informal upward flow of information. In the late 1970s the Pittown plant had one of the worst records for quality and productivity and one of the highest grievance loads in the corporation. The UAW local enjoyed a reputation as one of the most militant in the country.

Background to the Intervention

In 1977, the local union found itself on the verge of a wildcat strike over something it knew local management had no control over. The strike was only averted at the eleventh hour due to mediation by the national union. Officials of the local union experienced some remorse about their behavior and became willing to try and find a better way to relate to management. At first they tried to create a "forum for discussing common concerns," consisting of all union reps and all managers above a certain level. Such union-management "cooperation" was unheard of in Pittown; at the time, simply being seen in the plant's front office area was grounds for impeaching a union official. This soon degenerated, however, into ongoing collective bargaining and was dropped. Soon after, the plant manager was promoted and the new plant manager approached the union and convinced them to go on a trip to see what was happening at another United Automotive plant that was receiving media attention for its Quality of Work Life (QWL) program. The three top managers and three local union leaders went for a four-day trip to look at the plant.

This trip was highly successful, not only in convincing them that a different way of operating was possible but in allowing for better personal relations to develop among them. As one of the union stewards put it, the trip allowed them to spend time together over a few beers and size each other up. During this trip, a sense of respect and trust between the plant manager and the shop chairman began to develop.

Upon returning home they decided to set up a steering committee consisting of the entire local union bargaining committee and an equal number of senior managers. Having learned from their prior experience, they agreed that none of the issues normally dealt with through collective bargaining would be brought into the meetings. Union leaders were very hesitant to commit to anything fearing that they would be seen "in bed with management." There were different caucuses that vied for power at each election and the opposing caucus was certain to disparage the change effort at the next election. In general, senior managers agreed that union officials had more to lose from attempting cooperation than did management. The plant manager stated his belief that it was up to management to make the first move, but he sure wanted to feel the union right behind him.

They were not sure what to do next and decided to look inside the plant for a place where the right combination of people existed to "try a new way of working." The committee decided to sanction an experiment in one assembly department where a young department head and a union steward had developed an unusually good relationship. The department head, Bob, and the union steward, Joe, proposed to meet with all the workers and supervisors in one area (the fastener line) and solicit their input. The fastener line was known as one of the worst areas in the plant for grievances, absenteeism, and poor quality. Just a few weeks prior, workers had dropped a fire extinguisher down three stories through the roof of a supervisor's car. They believed that if improvements could be made in this department, it would be very visible and convincing to the rest of the plant. The steering committee agreed to this and decided that attendance at meetings would be voluntary and that workers would be paid overtime for meetings.

When Bob and Joe began holding the meetings, the workers sat passively through them. After a few meetings they finally spoke up, demanding the removal of the supervisors. This Bob would not do. Then they demanded tools and equipment to make their jobs easier. These Bob supplied. Then Bob asked them to redesign the layout of the fastener line in whatever way made the most sense to them. This they eagerly did. After four months, drastic improvements in worker attitudes, product quality, and absenteeism were observed. Relations between the workers and supervisors were the best they'd ever been. Two months later, Bob was promoted to production manager (number-two man).

One of Bob's first acts as production manager was to call a meeting of all middle and senior managers in the plant and tell them that they must get involved in improving the quality of work life in the plant or they would no longer have a job. The main, initial effect of this was to create a great deal of resentment among the department heads, most of whom were senior to Bob. They saw this as a "sell-out to the union."

Meanwhile in the steering committee, a guiding vision for the changes was being formulated, though not in any formal way. It was a vision that was never formally announced or put on wall plaques, yet years later it would be spontaneously enunciated during interviews by employees all over this large facility. This vision boiled down to an agreement between senior managers and union leaders that: "(1) everybody should enjoy coming to work, and (2) we're going to stop hassling each other over the 5 percent who are troublemakers and start looking after the 95 percent who just want a decent job."

Also at this time, the steering committee began discussing the need for full-time internal change agents to facilitate the effort. They chose Joe, the union steward, and Bert, one of the middle managers who had been involved in the fastener-line experiment. Out of that experience they developed the following intervention strategy.

Parallel Structure Creation

Joe and Bert would wait until invited by a department head to begin a QWL process in his or her department. They would begin by giving feedback on the head's management style, emphasize the need to be less authoritarian, and provide coaching throughout the process. Once convinced the department head was ready, they would facilitate a series of meetings, including the department head, his or her general supervisors, and the shop stewards responsible for the department. These meetings consisted mainly of intergroup conflict-resolution techniques, where past grievances were aired, a common vision of what QWL meant was developed, and an agreement to cooperate was made. In these meetings, Joe and Bert emphasized the development of shared leadership and consensus decision making. Once this group was functioning well, general supervisors were asked whether they would like to have the same kind of meetings with their supervisors. By this point in the process, general supervisors were usually eager to do so. Generals, supervisors, and union stewards would meet and, using the same techniques, work with the group until it developed into a cohesive unit. Then supervisors were asked if they'd like to meet with their workers, and once more a series of meetings were facilitated until the groups were working well on their own, and then Joe and Bert would leave. This "waterfalling" intervention resulted in the development of a parallel learning structure in each department they worked in. As shown in Fig. 5.1, the resulting structure had three layers of groups, integrated by union stewards and linking pin managers.

During this change project, Joe and Bert noticed an interesting process that seemed to play out consistently with groups, no matter what the level of the hierarchy. When groups first started meeting, subordinates would sit passively and say very little. Joe and Bert would exhort them to speak up. After a few such meetings, the superior in the group would be asked by a subordinate to do something. Often these were simple housekeeping matters, or the procurement of some work-related item. Joe and Bert coached the superior to pay attention to this event, to commit clearly to doing something and then make sure to do it. People were often amazed when the superior actually did what he or she had said. At the next meeting, subordinates would finally open up and express their resentment and bitterness for past transgressions. Interestingly, union stewards often played an important, supportive role in that they were much less hesitant to point out flaws in the superior's management style. Joe and Bert would coach the superior to expect this "revolt" and counsel him or her to sit through it passively and take the heat. In almost all cases, at the meeting following the revolt the group would get down to business and begin addressing work-related problems.

When subordinates made requests, it was often for something that required the help of skilled trades or the maintenance department. As in most older factories, these two departments had more work than they could handle. Having been by and large left out of the QWL process, they treated managers' requests as no different from any others. The result was that some managers were not able to respond to group requests for a long time, and group members

Figure 5.1
The Parallel Learning Structure at Pittown Plant

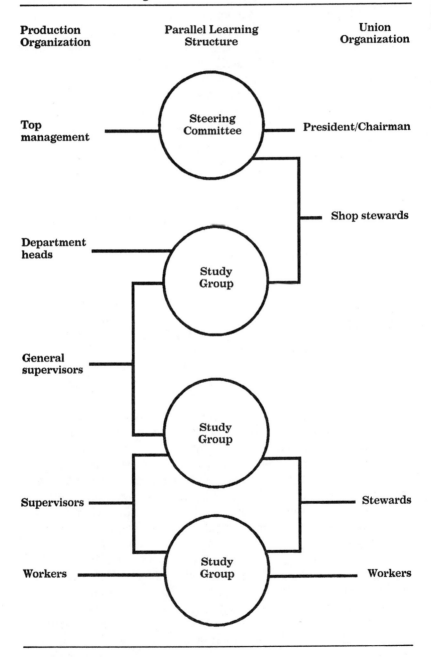

saw this as a lack of commitment on the part of the manager. Once Joe and Bert realized what was going on, the steering committee's clout was used to inform the service departments about the special nature of group requests and attention to them speeded up.

Diffusion of the Parallel Structure

At first it was difficult to get more than a couple of department heads to participate. They resented the pressure from Bob to get involved and particularly resented the fact that they weren't allowed to begin a QWL process without the involvement of Joe, the union steward. Prior to becoming pro-QWL, Joe had been one of the most zealous in his humiliation tactics. After a couple of off-site meetings between the local union and department heads, one of the most senior department heads (Frank Sturk) decided to try it out. Frank was famous throughout the plant for his abusive treatment of subordinates, and his name was used in the local slang to connote a highly unreasonable, authoritarian person (as in "what a sturk"). A year later Frank was to admit that he originally went along to please his boss, not really believing anything would come of it. What happened was that the process worked, Frank's department started to come alive, and Frank became a symbol of the "new way."

At first few union officials were willing to embrace this new way of working. Union reps faced elections every two years, and most believed that a big part of getting elected was having a reputation for being able to humiliate managers. The shop chairman and Joe were able to convince a few to at least attend meetings in the parallel learning structure. Many union reps were surprised to find out how bad relations within management were and how difficult it was for managers to exercise any kind of authority or influence the system that they, supposedly, managed. Through these meetings, union reps (and later, workers) developed a better appreciation for the inertia of the system and came to realize that many broken promises and reneged agreements from the past had been outside of management's control. As meetings progressed and the intervention diffused, caution turned to enthusiasm for virtually all those who were willing to participate. And their participation encouraged others to try it out as well.

Changes Emanating from the Intervention

Approximately two years after the first experiment on the fastener line, about half of the departments in this very large plant had fully elaborated parallel learning structures in place. Most of these groups had appointed leaders who were not the highest-ranking manager in the room and groups were using consensus decision making. In these departments, managers, union officials, and workers were euphoric about the changes. A number of supervisors and union officials described themselves as "teams who look after the people, and the people look after the product." Workers were now fixing problems rather than creating problems. Groups were cleaning up poor practices that had gone on for years. In the parallel learning structure, union officials were now gaining access to operating information that had been restricted from supervisors prior to the change. Managers were doing less fire-fighting and more planning. Workers were being asked to redesign tools and layouts on new, incoming work. After two years, the plant saw a 60 percent reduction in filed grievances, down to an average 2 percent of the work force. The labor-relations staff became alarmed at the steep reduction in their work and issued a memo reinforcing the use of official grievance procedures. This was ignored. From being the worst in the division, Pittown became one of the top two plants in quality and efficiency, exceeding efficiency standards by 8 percent.

Analysis and Some Learnings from the Case

There is a great deal to be learned from Pittown about developing cooperative labor-management relations. Here we'll focus mainly on the issues involved in implementing parallel learning structures and try to understand what is helpful about them. Other aspects of this case pertinent to the issues of developing cooperative labor-management relations are available elsewhere.[2]

A very helpful perspective for looking at this case is that afforded by intergroup relations theory.[3] Factories, like all organizations, are made up of multiple groups. In addressing labor-management relations, people tend to treat these as the two major groups involved. This is a mistake. As the Pittown case shows, there

---

2. Bushe (1988a).

3. This section draws from the theories of Dahrendorf (1959), Gamson (1968), Oshry (1977, 1980, 1988), Smith (1982), and Alderfer (1987). In our consulting we have found Gamson and Oshry's work particularly useful.

were a lot of different groups with different perspectives on the change process. There were different factions within the union—both the formal caucuses and informal groupings with different points of view. Within management, there was a group of department heads that resented senior management's actions, and there was hostility toward superiors at most levels of management. In fact, the case description given above simplified the real situation greatly. Boundaries between service and assembly departments, between the two assembly units, between shifts, between workers and the union, between the plant and divisional staffs, all created issues that had to be dealt with at Pittown. Below we'll look at three aspects of intergroup relations pertinent to Pittown's parallel learning structure intervention: boundaries and fault lines, power configurations, and different power sources for tops, middles, and bottoms.

Boundaries and Fault Lines

Paying attention to boundaries between formal and informal groups is a key part of any large-scale intervention in bureaucracies. Where boundaries are fairly permeable, people generally know and understand one another; information flow is less distorted, and there is more opportunity for mutual influence. The less permeable the boundaries between groups, the less information flow and the more distortions in the pictures they have of each other. The most critical boundaries are ones we call "fault lines." Fault lines are found where two or more groups habitually point fingers at each other, claiming that any problem is the other group's fault. Like fault lines in the earth's crust, these are boundaries where a lot of pressure and heat has built up over time, with the potential for rapid transformation of the entire surrounding geography (and, unfortunately, the potential to swallow up anyone who happens to be in the wrong place at the wrong time). The boundary between union and management tends to be a fault line.

The parallel learning structure is especially useful in developing better labor-management relations because it can address so many boundaries simultaneously. Organizations with poor labor relations tend also to have poor relations within the managerial ranks. Why should middle managers treat the union or workers any better than they are being treated by their superiors? Interventions into labor-management relations that do not also address poor relations within management (and also, perhaps, in the union) are probably doomed to failure. As was seen in Pittown, the formation of the parallel learning structure provided an opportunity to heal old wounds within the managerial ranks as well as between union and management.

Some managers, realizing this, put off working on labor-management relations until work is done within the management ranks. There is probably some wisdom in this, but there may be a big opportunity lost. At Pittown, one of the things that first brought middle managers and union reps together was that they could agree on the flaws in the senior managers' operating style. It is not clear whether middle managers would have been as forthcoming in their resentments if there hadn't been union reps with nothing to lose in the meetings willing to say hard things to the "boss." On the other side, learning that managers had a lot of beefs with each other helped to allay union fears of being co-opted by a unified, overwhelming management juggernaut. In this latter instance, we see one aspect of the process of development in intergroup relations. Where boundaries are hard, pictures of other groups tend to be simple generalizations with little appreciation for individual differences within the "other group." In such cases, people talk as if all workers are lazy and uncaring or all managers are overly controlling and stupid. One milestone of development in intergroup relations is when people begin to differentiate members of the "other group," as in Pittown, where union reps began to see different managers as different people, and vice versa.

In relations between groups in organizations, certain conditions are more likely to lead to fault lines. One is when subgroups have very different operating cultures because of the very different nature of their tasks. For example, people in R & D and people in sales tend to see each other in distorted ways because their subcultures are so different. Another is when different groups' goals are in competition with each other. For example, maintenance departments are trying to minimize repair time, while manufacturing departments are trying to maximize machine maintenance in order to minimize lost production time. A very important determinant of fault lines is the power relations between groups.

Power Configurations

It is very difficult for two groups with highly unequal power to be able to see each other very clearly. Furthermore, the way in which the most powerful group uses its power over the less powerful will have a big effect. In industrial organizations, senior managers are the most powerful because of their legitimate authority and because they have the most control over valued resources. Senior managers are trying to get employees to perform a set of predictable, reliable behaviors without any face-to-face interaction. The options for such "social control" are fairly limited. The most divisive means for management to attempt to control workers (or supervisors) is to insulate them from access to decision making or other resources that might decrease management's "authority." The use of coercion (threats) isn't much better. Both means tend to create impermeable boundaries, reinforce the power differentials, and engender distorted images of the other group. Insulation also forces those with less power to use such tactics as sabotage, illegal walkouts, or harassment to influence those with more power.

Somewhat less divisive is the use of rewards or inducements by those with power to "buy" reliable performance. Though this is the ideal of Western business practice, we have been in very few organizations where, outside of the sales staff, people have a sense of being rewarded for any behavior at all. In factories, with their tight interdependencies, it is virtually impossible to isolate rewardable behaviors, and this problem is compounded by union contracts based on seniority and not merit. Where inducements are used for social control, groups tend not to be aggressively distrustful toward one another, but there isn't much trust either. Rather, people act out of self-interest, and can't be expected to perform unless there is something in it for them.

The final method of social control available to senior managers is to seek common purpose with those with less power and to create forums where everyone has access to decision making. Such "participation" creates more permeable boundaries between groups and increases trust between them. This relation between means of social control and trust appears to work both ways. The more those at the top (tops) insulate those at the bottom (bottoms), the more they come to distrust one another. The more they distrust one another, the more they will use insulation and coercion to influence each other. On the other hand, the more tops and bottoms trust each other, the more tops will use participation for control and the more bottoms will participate in order to influence tops. The more they interact in making decisions that affect them both, the more they come to trust each other. Methods of control by tops, of influence by bottoms, and the trust between them tend to form stable, self-perpetuating, power configurations. Intervention into these power configurations requires either a change in control and influence tactics or a change in trust. Movement from insular/coercive power configurations to participative/trusting configurations is an incremental process of opening boundaries, taking a risk successfully, and thereby engendering more trust to open boundaries a little more.

At Pittown, the parallel structure created an ongoing, weekly forum where union and management, and different levels of management, could experiment with opening their boundaries to develop trust. The parallel learning structure was an opportunity for those with less power to participate in forums for decision making. But at first, distrusting tops, bottoms would simply sit passively and not participate. The initial request to the senior manager in each group was crucial in testing the sincerity of the manager and in engendering enough trust to enable subordinates to speak up. As each risk was taken successfully (and in a few cases they weren't, causing group regression), more trust was built. As more trust was built, the possibility of true cooperation increased. The use of consensus decision making and shared leadership further helped to reduce power differences between group members. While power differences could never be eliminated, their distorting effects were minimized.

Developing System Power

Some people think of power as a zero sum quantity; that is, that one can only increase his or her power at the expense of someone else. In some very limited cases this is true. This is not true in organizations, however. Research has shown that in effective organizations, all members feel that they can influence the organization in matters directly affecting them. In fact, bottoms in effective organizations may describe themselves as more influential than tops in ineffective ones.[4] Simply being at the top is no guarantee that one feels "powerful." Yet the amount of potential system power in an organization is, for all practical purposes, unlimited. *System power is the capacity to influence a system for its own good, to help one's system survive and grow.*

---

4. Tannenbaum (1968).

Many managers at Pittown were initially afraid that they would be giving away power to the union and losing control. This is a common reaction from managers when a QWL process begins. After the groups began functioning well, these managers found that they had more ability to influence the organization than they had ever had. It was as though they had to give away power in order to gain power. How does such a paradox occur?

One answer is that as relations between superiors and subordinates improved, the amount of legitimacy superiors had to use their authority increased as well. People had more trust and respect for their boss and were more willing to do what he or she said. This is far from the whole answer, however. To understand the profound effect of the parallel learning structure on system power at Pittown, we have to understand the potential for system power embedded in various groups in hierarchical organizations.[5]

Any hierarchy can be usefully thought of as having three key groups—tops, middles, and bottoms. This is obviously a simplification of reality, and we will deal with it very briefly here. Tops are the people who control the resources and have the authority to make policies that guide the system. Bottoms are the people who actually do the work of the system, producing goods or services. Middles are the people who manage and supervise the work of others and are the information conduit between tops and bottoms. These positions are always *relative* to others. In different situations, an individual can be a top, a middle, or a bottom. In an organization, the lines between these three groups tend to be fairly clear. Each group has sources of system power unique to it. The main ways in which tops influence the survival and growth of their systems is through *(1) developing a vision or mission that captures the excitement of system members, and (2) creating structures that make it possible for system members to devote their energies to that vision.* At Pittown, tops manifested their system power through developing a vision of a new way of working and through sanctioning the creation of parallel learning structures.

Bottoms are the only group in the unique position to *optimize work processes.* This is their source of system power. They do this by

---

5. This section is based on the work of Oshry (1977, 1980, 1988) and Smith (1982).

investing their energy into work processes (because they think they're good, right, or proper) or by withholding their effort and highlighting what needs to be corrected. The intervention at Pittown succeeded in turning a work force that had been passively aggressive (or outright stuck on rebelling) into one willing to become involved and willing to voice what problems needed attention.

But the biggest effect of the parallel learning structure on system power was on the middles. Middles are the system integrators. The unique source of system power for middles is the opportunity to *influence the communication and interaction patterns between all parts of the system,* through being responsive to tops and bottoms while maintaining independence from them. Because of their middleness, middles typically know more about the real state of their systems than either tops or bottoms do. They are also in the best position to distribute this information and coordinate various parts of the system. Middles exercise their system power when they influence different parts of the system to act in a coordinated manner, enhancing rather than interfering with the total system.

The unique dilemma of middles is being torn in so many directions. This "diffusion" can be their source of power or their downfall. It is their source of power when they use their wide-ranging knowledge and contacts to integrate the system. It's their downfall when they try to cope by aligning themselves and losing their independent stance. Middles can become *stuck-up* (aligned with tops) or *stuck-down* (aligned with bottoms). When they do this, they are no longer in the middle, and their unique source of system power as integrators is lost. Middles' system power is also dissipated by becoming *stuck-in-the-middle,* trying to respond to both tops' and bottoms' demands. Without taking an independent stance, such middles get torn apart in a hectic, frenzied work pace and lose their potential source of system power. These well-intentioned people are the most likely to burn out and experience stress-related illnesses.

On the other hand, middles can be too independent to the point of being totally nonresponsive. Being nonresponsive by withholding services, generating complex procedures, and discouraging the intrusion of others may help middles cope with conflicting pressures, but in doing so they lose all their potential for system power.

Middles tap into their system power by:

1. developing an independent perspective while remaining responsive to tops and bottoms,
2. creating time for reflection so that they aren't submerged by the demands of others, and
3. developing networks with other middles.

Some people argue that system integration can only be achieved through middles' networking. Networking for middles is a critical but poorly understood source of system power. This is what the parallel structure provides that changes the shape of system power in a factory—a place for middles to network. At Pittown, this networking brought together two unlikely sets of middles—union reps and managers. They discovered that together they had far more access to information that allowed them to act for the system's own good. This was not only good for the system, it also helped these individuals meet their own goals. Union reps were able to provide a better workplace for their people and get faster responses to their ideas and complaints. Managers were able to build better cars more efficiently.

One of the ironies of middleness is that middles will often resist networking. Generally, if you ask middles if they want to join another group, they'll say no. There are many possible reasons for this. One is that middles may fear that the "network" will be one more competing demand pulling at them. Another is that they feel they have no time due to the hectic pace and pressure from tops and bottoms. Middles also tend to identify more with the groups they service than with their peers, and job definitions and reward structures often promote tension and competitiveness between middles. Another reason why middles don't network is that meeting alone can cause a backlash from tops who are frightened and experience themselves as having low power.

We can see that at Pittown, the changes allowed people to exercise the unique opportunities their positions gave them for system power. Bottoms were able to abandon their rebellious position because they now had access to forums where they could point out where work processes needed fixing and get responses. Tops worked at developing a vision and found some way to communicate it and developed a structure to support the implementation of that vision. Perhaps most importantly, middles (managers and union reps) were able to network, discard their roles as antagonists, and spend time integrating the system.

Summary

The following list of issues to attend to in developing cooperative labor-management relations is not intended to be exhaustive. Rather, it is intended to highlight things to pay attention to when using a parallel learning structure intervention. In general, the development of cooperative labor-management relations requires a recognition that "labor-management" is only one of a number of boundaries between groups in factories who are distrustful and hostile to one another. Successful attempts to engender real cooperation on the shop floor require paying attention to most if not all of the "fault lines" in the organization simultaneously. The greatest strength of the parallel learning structure for this task is that it allows hostility within levels of management to be addressed at the same time as hostility between labor and management is addressed.

Key Points in Using Parallel Learning Structures to Develop Cooperative Labor-Management Relations

1. Keep initial goals of the project ambiguous. Parallel learning structures are the technostructural side of the intervention. Just as important is the vision that tells people what the purpose of the structure is. One of the main ways past rivals come together to cooperate is through agreement on some higher purpose or common goals. Quality of Work Life has been very successful as a common goal in bringing union and management leaders together. One of the reasons it has been successful is its ambiguity. Because of its vague, benign quality, people are willing "to take a bite and see what it tastes like." When past adversaries begin a process of developing cooperation, it is almost never phrased as such. Part of what gives them their identities is their opposition. Furthermore, few if any enter into such a project fully committed. Rather, they enter with caution, and often with pessimism. Under such conditions, it is premature to try and define what

QWL means, or in the case of Pittown, what "a new way of working" means. What it "means" can only be discovered in the process of doing it. Out of that process a clearer sense of vision emerges. Defining a vision, especially among past adversaries, should be a living, iterative process, not a set of guidelines carved in stone and hung on the wall.

2. If a process is going to create labor-management cooperation it must be a joint process from the outset. Initially, this means paying a lot of attention to ensuring that there is equal responsibility and equal say in all aspects of the process. The need for so much attention to this lessens as people come to trust one another.

3. When the process begins, it is very important that the top leaders of both union and management sit on the steering committee. Creating vertical-slice steering committees with representatives from all levels of the organization is nice in theory, but in practice it signals that this effort need not be taken too seriously. At first the steering committee is going to have to make policy decisions and commit resources that only the most senior managers and union officials have the authority to do. Once the parallel learning structure is in place and functioning well, the steering committee's task changes to a more integrative, operational role. At this time, it may be appropriate to reform the steering committee into a more representative vertical-slice committee.

4. Use a waterfall intervention, by production department. In bureaucratic factories, people are grouped by function and their main identification tends to be with the departments they are in. Also, it tends to be only at the department-head level that any significant decision-making authority exists. Therefore, it seems to work best to set up parallel learning structures *by department*. In practice, this means setting up a series of fairly independent structures throughout the plant. If the need for greater integration arises, people are very adept at finding ways to network these structures together. In setting up the parallel learning structure, it seems to work best by starting at the top of the department and working downward,

one group at a time, creating a cascading flow, or "waterfall," effect. By sitting in the initial meetings with their boss, managers and supervisors develop an appreciation for what their subordinates will feel when it is their turn to start their groups. At Pittown, supervisors who were initially opposed to worker participation couldn't wait to start their groups once they had a chance to participate themselves with their own superiors.

5. Be prepared to respond to group ideas. Once the group is functioning well, it will naturally turn to the topic that concerns everyone: work. Groups will develop ideas for how to improve work that may require few or many resources and may affect few or many others. In practice, requests for information, action, and/or resources should only go as high up in the hierarchy as the lowest manager with authority to respond. One of the surest ways to paralyze such a parallel learning structure is to require that all group ideas and requests funnel through the senior steering committee. In cases where implementation of a group's idea requires few resources and will affect few others, groups should be able to execute on their own authority. Where it will affect others, those others should be brought into the decision-making loop.

Some people argue that groups must develop their own tasks. This is probably true at first, but after a while groups are usually glad to have someone in a senior position point out what the big-ticket problems are, and often see this as a sign that senior managers care about and value the group.

There is a balance here between providing too much direction prematurely, on the one hand, and, on the other, appearing to not care about what the groups do.

6. Service departments, especially maintenance and skilled trades, have a critical role to play in the initial formation of parallel learning structures in unionized factories. As we saw in Pittown, one of the first tests of a manager's sincerity by workers is to ask for something to be fixed. Most union contracts specify who is allowed to fix it, so the manager has no recourse but to depend on maintenance or skilled trades to respond in a timely manner.

If they don't respond quickly, workers will perceive this as proof that the manager isn't sincere and will settle into their pessimism. Where there are problems between service and production departments, service departments should be educated about their important role in the change process and senior managers should monitor their execution of this role.

6

Transitional Structure Toward Sociotechnical System Design

All organizations are, by definition, sociotechnical systems. Most organizations, however, have not taken this fact into account in their design. In practice, most organizations are designed to maximize the technical subsystem while ignoring the social subsystem. Sociotechnical system design principles seek "joint optimization" of both the social and technical subsystems with their environment. As a result, sociotechnical systems (STS) theory-based designs are significantly different from traditional organizational designs. At the most basic level, traditional organizational design involves specialized and simple jobs, hierarchical control, centralized authority, individual rewards, segmentation of activities, faith in technical solutions, maintenance of the status quo, buffering from the environment, and an undervaluing of human resources. STS design, on the other hand, is centered around a valuing of human resources, whole and complex jobs, worker autonomy, delegated authority, group and system rewards, elimination of barriers between functions and levels, human and technical solutions, concern with innovation, and attention to the environment.

Sociotechnical systems theory has been the basis for a number of important breakthroughs in organizational design. Yet, the majority of the successful applications of STS design have been in new facilities. The principles and corresponding practices of STS appear to be significantly different from conventional organizational design, so much so that the redesign of existing facilities is a very complex task with few documented successes.[1]

Military organizations typify traditional organizational design: They are highly structured, inflexible, and hierarchical bureaucracies in which individuals are commanded to perform like machines and are treated with no more respect than interchangeable parts.[2] But the American military, like other organizations today, faces complex challenges in accomplishing its mission in a rapidly changing technological, social, economic, and political environment. The constraints of the military culture, powerful leadership, and bureaucracy, war and peace dynamics, and general resistance to change make planned change a major challenge, but they also provide a rigorous test of the utility of parallel learning structures for redesigning organizations using STS theory as the underlying framework.

Case: The Military Data Processing Unit

"It's not working. We need that information now, not tomorrow!" Such might have been the comment of a general waiting for reports from the military data processing unit (DPU). A new system had been installed, and instead of improving data processing capabilities and output between units across the continent, it seemed to obstruct communication. The DPU was not getting its vital job done.

Located on the outskirts of a cosmopolitan European city, the buildings and grounds appeared to be a basic government operation. Once inside the gates, however, one found a U.S. military data processing unit, which provided a vital communication link between military units regarding military operations and readiness across the Continent. The organization achieved its purpose by using a highly sophisticated technology for data collection and processing. There were approximately 150 people stationed at the unit at any time. Most individuals were on a three-year tour of duty, so the composition of personnel was continually changing. The primary demand

---

1. See Trist (1981), Cummings (1986), Pava (1986), and Pasmore (1988).

2. Saborosky, Thompson, and McPherson (1982).

made on personnel was that of security. Tight security measures were employed on both the unit's military and civilian personnel, especially in the buildings housing the computers. Even though the function of the DPU was extremely vital, the unit was described by some as having a "country-club" atmosphere. Personnel did not perceive much pressure to meet deadlines, and did not push themselves to produce.

The unit consisted of two distinct customer/product oriented divisions, a separate group of highly skilled systems analysts, a comparatively less skilled group of computer operators, and various staff departments. Technical personnel were highly trained in advanced data processing techniques. The additional experience and advanced training provided at this location, as well as the beauty of the area itself, made assignments attractive.

A Commanding Officer (CO), positioned at the top of the organizational hierarchy, assumed full authority and responsibility for the unit. This CO tended to remove himself from personal interaction with his subordinates. Personnel were highly sensitive to the CO, and reacted strongly to his actions. The CO desired to improve productivity and was disturbed by the relaxed country-club atmosphere. He was determined to change the unit and people's perceptions of it.

The CO and the rest of the unit did share concerns about the new computer technology. The operators had used the older system for some time, and their familiarity with it had contributed to the relaxed atmosphere. The recent installation of the modern computer system appeared to create many problems for the operators, and these problems were compounded when computer parts mysteriously vanished or malfunctioned. Specialists from the manufacturer were sent to the site to assist the operators in adapting to the new technology, but DPU personnel were hostile to these outsiders, and did not respond to their aid. The new system functioned well in the presence of these specialists, yet in their absence, it malfunctioned. It was clear that some direct action had to be taken to resolve this problem, because the new system could not be used effectively in this condition. In the mean time, the armed forces headquarters was depending on data provided by the unit under strict time deadlines. Nine months after assuming his new position, the CO decided to request some outside aid in order to discover the root of the problem and make the new system operational. The military (via the Army

Research Institute as the sponsor) complied with his request, and as a result this project emerged.[3]

Initial Entry

The initial phase of scanning and contracting was guided by the CO, an internal consultant who was a part of the Army Research Institute and was the champion behind using STS theory, and the outside consultants. The initial inquiry process consisted of a series of meetings and individual interviews with all levels of management and employees in order to fully scan the DPU. During this process, the consultant team was also attempting to create and set in motion a learning climate and co-inquiry process. The meetings combined an education process (about the project and potential areas of further work) with group discussions that generated data. Open discussions about concerns over this project were encouraged, but not all personnel felt free to voice their opinions. This guarded openness was purportedly a reflection of the unit's military culture.

At a feedback meeting senior officers/managers in the organization discussed the initial scanning document that was prepared by the consultant team. Various ways to proceed with the project were explored. The managers decided to implement a transitional mechanism using a parallel learning structure to facilitate a sociotechnical assessment and redesign. Some members of the consultant team were concerned that the project was unrealistic and would fail. Their uneasiness stemmed from: (1) their lack of familiarity with the organizational culture; (2) an unclear level of support from the various levels of management; and (3) the inherent contradictions between the culture of a parallel learning structure and that of a bureaucratic, military organization. The CO's strong personal determination to proceed, along with his feeling that there was much to gain and little to lose by the experiment, provided the needed impetus to convince the consultant team to proceed.

Parallel Structure Creation

A steering committee was created, composed of the CO, three of his immediate subordinates, and individuals representing the technical and social subsystems of the organization. Its members were all

---

3. Bill Pasmore was the lead consultant/researcher on the project. See Pasmore, Shani, and Mietus (1982).

managers in the DPU. The CO informed members of their additional duties at one of the management team meetings. In spite of good intentions, a discussion of roles, assumptions, functions, and expectations did not take place.

The parallel learning structure ultimately consisted of four groups—the steering committee, the consulting team, and two study groups. The initial goal was to create a microcosm of the entire unit Its formation required clear criteria for the creation of each of the groups and careful coordination and communication with the unit and the larger, Army organization. The steering committee decided to form two study groups in order to involve more organization members in the change process. The two groups received training, team-building input, and process guidance from the consultants. Each group had approximately ten members. Membership in the study groups was determined by the CO and the steering committee. Their composition was established to be one-third top management, one-third middle management, and one-third workers and included both military and civilian personnel. For coordination, control, and communication purposes, each study group contained at least two members from the steering committee. Selected individuals were notified and ordered to attend. Participation was not voluntary, although some adjustments were made three months later to allow highly interested individuals to join groups.

Two organizational briefings were held in order to communicate to the entire DPU before the study groups met. The goals of the project and some potential activities were discussed. Organization members were briefed on the formation of the study groups and the steering committee, as well as on the decisions leading to their creation. The selection process was described, and the CO invited everyone to participate in the study groups' activities, either by providing ideas to the study group members or by accepting an open invitation to observe any of the forthcoming study group meetings.

A general off-site meeting of the parallel learning structure (steering committee, study groups, and consultants) occurred the next day. The meeting was conducted by the consultants and the CO. It began with a discussion of the process that had taken place to date, including the process and criteria for choosing group members. The roles, functions, and potential tasks of the different parts of the parallel learning structure were defined through role clarification activities. Some suggestions for potential activities of the parallel learning structure were made by the consultants. A time frame was set for the overall intervention effort. During the meeting the consultants were struck by the limited interaction that took place between group members, an observation that reinforced some of their initial fears.

The study groups met weekly. More frequent sessions were scheduled when the external consultants were on site. While the internal consultant was on site most of the time, attended all of the parallel structure activities, and was available for any additional help, he was also involved with other military units. The parallel learning structure meetings progressed over time from being consultant-led to being more self-directed. As the more self-directing culture of the parallel learning structure took hold, study groups began to generate their own agendas and ideas. It wasn't until the groups began analyzing data, about six months into the project, that they became fully self-directing.

One of the factors affecting the ability of the study groups to develop a co-inquiry culture was the reluctance of military personnel to accept civilians in their midst. Civilians, including representatives of the computer company and noncommissioned officers, were considered "outsiders." It was difficult for them to gain the respect of the commissioned officers. In the event of military crises, the civilians were not to take part in any military maneuvers. That meant to some of the officers that the civilians were not really a part of the unit, since "we are here to be ready for combat." This created tension as the military depended on civilians to keep the unit in constant readiness for action that the civilians would not take part in. Some of the officers respected only those with combat experience (many of the officers had spent some time in Vietnam).

Nevertheless, as group members worked together through the early tasks, the value of each individual's input became apparent, and both the military and the civilian personnel gained some more respect for each other and eventually began to accept one another. The study group's experience generating the list of questions for the interviews (described below) was especially helpful in breaking down the barriers. During a "discussion" of clustering and rank ordering the list of questions, the underlying tensions between an officer and a civilian finally surfaced. By switching roles and arguing each other's point of view, they saw, for the first time, what they were putting each other through. Of course, each represented views held by others in the group, so this exchange, which was basically an "us-versus-them" issue, had an emotional effect on everyone in the group. The role-playing activity and the discussions that followed did much to reduce the barriers between the military and the civilian personnel and moved the group much closer to an ideal culture for co-inquiry.

Inquiry Phase

The first function of the parallel learning structure was to gather information about the organization within a sociotechnical systems conceptual framework. Prerequisite to this work was the education of the parallel learning structure members in sociotechnical system theory and methods. Time restraints limited a lengthy educational process. Two and a half days were spent learning about the basic STS theory, design principles, and approach to change. Specific training in analytical methods was planned for a later stage as the project progressed. The parallel learning structure was to collect data about the social and technical systems and the organization's interaction with its environment. After exploring different data-collection methodologies, and based upon the recommendations of the consultants, a variety of data-gathering techniques were chosen. A survey questionnaire, interview guide, and guide to task analysis were developed. The first two focused on social system issues and involved all organization members. The guide to task analysis emphasized the technical system.

The survey was designed primarily by the consulting team, with final modifications by the study groups. Completion by DPU personnel was voluntary, and responses were kept anonymous. Approximately 70 percent of the unit's members completed the survey. The majority of individuals who did not complete the survey were absent from the site at the time. The resulting data indicated that DPU members were neutral to positive in their perceptions of the climate of the organization and its various internal processes. They were generally satisfied with the design of their jobs, and were slightly motivated and wanted to do a good job. For the most part, they were positive regarding their supervisors' style and competence. Their attitudes toward work group processes were generally positive. While they indicated keen interest in improving their technical skills, the strength of their needs for growth and challenge through the work itself was only average. The trouble spots identified included dissatisfaction with planning and scheduling, lack of teamwork, lack of intergroup communication, overemphasis of rank over technical ability, and lack of meaningful performance standards.

The interview guide was developed by asking the study groups to generate a list of interview questions they felt would highlight the organization's social system and some of the issues not covered in the survey. From this list the consulting team developed the interview guide itself. The interviews were designed to fulfill two purposes: (1) gather information about the organization, and (2) better inform organizational members about the study in hopes of winning their support and involvement in the change process. The interviews lasted approximately one hour and, due to the strong recommendation by parallel structure members, were conducted by the consultants. The results of the interview process were diverse. Major dissatisfactions included communications problems, lack of cooperation across boundaries, intergroup conflict, lack of uniform practices, problems with supervision, and relations with users. Concerns were expressed about some groups receiving unfair treatment and a lack of clear performance measures. Similarly, it was felt that the reward system was inadequate; that is, it was difficult to identify individuals who were putting forth extra effort and those who were not.

The third major level of analysis was directed at the technical system. The purpose of this assessment was to identify problems or variances that occurred as members of the organization went about their work. After a long discussion within the parallel structure, the group decided that the individuals most qualified to carry out this analysis were middle-level managers. They reasoned that the middle managers were close enough to the problems experienced by members of the teams and at the same time had a broad perspective, which enabled them to see the connections among problems across team boundaries. So the steering committee asked the middle-management staff to do the analysis.

The method of technical system analysis used by most STS consultants was developed primarily for use in industrial settings, where the major transformation of materials from inputs to outputs is accomplished by machinery. In the Army, as well as in many other service-oriented organizations, the major transformation of materials from input into output is accomplished by people, sometimes through the application of highly specialized skills, knowledge, and sophisticated technology. The consulting team developed a task-analysis guide to begin the assessment of the technical system. It included the following elements:

1. An overview of the organization, with a focus on roles, requisite skills, and skill levels;
2. An assessment of the nature of the problems created by the way work was organized and the technology used by workers;
3. An assessment of the potential of jobs to satisfy and motivate the individuals performing them;
4. An overall assessment of an area's effectiveness at meeting formal goals; and
5. Manager recommendations for area and overall organizational improvement.

In order to assure consistency in completing the task-analysis guide, the middle-level managers met as a group. They were educated on how to perform the task analysis and on the basic theory and concepts behind its construction. The guide was broken into segments and treated sequentially at four meetings. The last part of the guide gathered data for the "variances analysis," which has been a standard method in STS analyses. Individuals received assistance and training from the consultants during these sessions and were then able to complete a detailed analysis of their technical system.

As the analysis phase progressed, the steering committee served several critical functions within the parallel learning structure and between the parallel structure and the formal organization. It was a communication link between upper management and the study groups. Keeping upper management up to date with the study's progress and dealing with the CO's needs to be actively involved in every activity and stage of the project required a lot of their energy. The steering committee set the direction for the study groups, decided on priorities, and added definition to project ideas. Its members performed leadership functions at the study group meetings. It acted as a buffer between the study groups and the larger organization, thereby keeping the unit productive and preventing overzealous study group activities. (For example, the working relationships between a few of the commanding officers and some of the civilians were very tense as each blamed the others for incompetence in understanding and operating the new technology. A few individuals in each of the study groups had attempted to make this issue the focus of the study. Furthermore, a rumor circulated that the study was actually a means of getting rid of unpopular managers. The steering committee had to step in and put the issue to rest by providing a clear statement that issues around working relationships were going to be only one of the areas to be examined in the study and not its main focus.)

Diagnostic Phase

Following the completion of these data-gathering processes, the parallel learning structure moved into the next phase of the process: making sense of the collected data and generating a shared understanding of the organization. The consultants fed all of the data collected from the organization back to the study groups, one piece at a time in raw form. The study group members were encouraged to develop a shared understanding of organizational reality and to identify problem areas in the organization. The survey, interviews, and technical analysis provided some indications of how the unit could operate more smoothly. However, the need for major change in the organization was not apparent to many of its personnel, nor was it desired. The parallel learning structure, and especially the study groups, addressed and began to explore the issues that emerged from the data. Many of these issues included the environmental context and its influence on the unit's effectiveness. They looked at unit design considerations from an STS perspective, and considered project definition, users' expectations of performance, ways to increase intergroup cooperation, organizational performance measures, the handling of security violations, rewards and recognition, and standard operating procedures.

Changes Emanating from the Parallel Structure

After becoming familiar with the data and developing a shared perception of organizational reality, the parallel learning structure was asked to generate a set of recommendations to improve overall unit performance. Although the data showed that most individuals were moderately happy with the unit, many of the customers and especially the military headquarters felt that the organization was functioning at a suboptimal level. Furthermore, through the sharing of the data it became apparent to parallel structure members that there were many areas that could be improved.

The first set of recommendations was relatively minor in scope, but extremely significant in gaining the trust of the employees. These recommendations included the requisition of a microwave oven for a lounge and the installation of carpeting in the computer room. The CO's prompt response to these requests (two weeks after a recommendation was made to the formal management group) demonstrated that employees could voice opinions and suggestions and see them implemented.

As these recommendations were acted upon, the energy level both within and outside the parallel learning structure changed. People realized for the first time that they could have a real impact on the unit. The parallel learning structure was actually able to function and change things without going through lengthy red tape. Ideas for change began to emerge from different parts of the organization and were channeled through the study group members. Some personnel even came to observe the study group meetings. The study group had to create a procedure to respond to and work through the ideas generated. The outcomes of the data analysis coupled with additional input resulted in five clusters of major recommendations emanating from the parallel learning structure:

1. Redesign of the organization based on STS principles. This cluster included suggestions on the formation of a matrix structure within the organization. Assignment flexibility and increased training for both line personnel and operators were key factors. Also included were the creation of a cross-unit planning committee and the addition of a Human Resources Manager to the organizational structure.

2. Development of new work teams. The focus of this cluster was to make work teams more efficient. Suggestions here were also consistent with STS theory. These suggestions included the assignment of systems analysts to teams, rotating programmers across teams, allowing groups to nominate project leaders, allowing teams to select, train, and evaluate their members, and making provisions for team work space.

3. Improvement of communication across the organization. Many of the suggestions made by the parallel learning

structure to improve communication dealt with feedback for work performed. These included: tying rewards to team performance, providing regular feedback on team performance, and holding reward/performance contracting meetings between supervisors and subordinates.

4. Development of productivity measures. These suggestions included developing measures by teams to aid in evaluation and recognition, and allowing teams to develop quality control standards and procedures for self-assessment.

5. Miscellaneous recommendations. There were a variety of recommendations in response to specific issues that had surfaced during the data-collection effort.

Of twenty-three major recommendations, eleven were accepted by the top-level management of the unit, four were rejected, and eight were returned to the study group for further study. This success rate, with nearly half of the initial recommendations accepted, was largely due to the commitment of the CO. Most of those suggestions that were not approved, such as altering the pay scale or modifying the performance-rating system, transcended the authority of the CO. As the top-level management of the formal unit was working through the recommendations with the steering committee, the parallel learning structure had an opportunity to work on a special project. The DPU was undergoing physical changes and relocation to a facility being constructed for them. The parallel learning structure was consulted to propose recommendations for the design of the facility. Within 45 days, the study groups completed a proposal that led to the ultimate design, including circular work stations that facilitated the development of work teams.

The issue of how best to implement the new organization design was discussed by both top management and the parallel learning structure. The external consultants were phasing out at this stage and the CO wanted to make sure that he was going to be in control of the actual formation of the new organization. An agreement was reached that the parallel structure would plan and execute the transition with approval of top management at every stage of the process. As the discussion was occurring, a few members of the parallel structure completed their tour of duty. This made it easier to merge the two study groups into one and for the CO (as was his wish), to become a full member of the study group.

The parallel learning structure then identified the following needs of the organization in the implementation process: (1) The organization needed help in the transitional phase between the "old way" and the "new way" of working. (2) The study groups needed help because they could not visualize the ideal organization they were trying to create. (3) The CO wanted to become a more integral part of the parallel learning structure. (4) The study group and top management team needed more structure and guidance from an internal consultant (the internal consultant was about to depart for another position in a different location). (5) The top-management team needed to continue to work on the recommendations of the study group. (6) The parallel learning structure needed more time to lay the necessary groundwork for the implementation of the changes recommended. The parallel structure then generated a list of tasks to be accomplished prior to implementing the recommended changes.

The task list included the following: (1) defining roles of organizational members under the proposed matrix structure; (2) developing procedures for selecting, staffing, and evaluating projects; (3) discussing policies and procedures for providing preferred assignments, training, and recognition for good performance; (4) redefining the continuing role of the study groups and their membership, including the selection and replacement mechanisms for members; (5) deciding how the groups and the top-management team would relate in the future; (6) developing procedures for the voluntary and mandatory movement of personnel within the matrix; and (7) discussing ways to incorporate users more closely into the program-development process. A timetable was set for the completion of these tasks, which would allow the implementation to take place by a certain date.

The CO, in turn, anticipated the upcoming organizational change to a matrix structure by revising the plans for the layout of the unit in ways that would make it easier for the teams to interact. He also laid out a rough sketch of his view of the organizational chart under the new matrix. Based on the discussions and recommendations of the parallel learning structure, a new chart was proposed. Also proposed were new role descriptions for members of the matrix organization and a general set of new policies and procedures. The new design was based on STS design principles. For example, it provided individuals with whole tasks and challenging jobs; multi-skilling was strongly encouraged, and ample training opportunities were provided for it; people were provided with a little more autonomy within the work teams; and cooperation across work teams was maximized. The implementation of the new organization came a month later.

As it was eventually implemented, the new design merged the two distinct project divisions into one under the direction of a project manager. The matrix also called for an added position of human resources manager, a position given equal stature to that of the project manager. This position was created to oversee quality assurance and the implementation of training and development of personnel. For the first time in the organization, human relations became as important as project completion. The parallel learning structure and top management considered this relatively new aspect of the organization to be an investment strategy because, at times, requests for service were turned down to provide the time and facilities for operator training sessions. They felt that though they were giving up immediate revenue, it would pay off in the long run with more highly trained operators capable of taking on more difficult assignments and a greater work load. Several improvements in performance were observed at the DPU over the course of the project. Six months after the implementation of the new organization design, the unit put in one of its best performances ever in its yearly exercise (controlled and monitored by people from headquarters). More users were trained to operate the system than ever before; more equipment was installed and maintained by organizational personnel; more programs and services were made available; and more people were assigned as troubleshooters in the field. Productivity per programmer showed an estimated 15 percent increase over the previous year. Users offered nothing but praise about the services provided, a significant contrast to previous performance evaluations. Furthermore, the CO was called upon to make only one small decision during the exercise, because others closer to the source of problems were making decisions and finding ways to implement them.

Although the performance of the unit showed improvement, employee attitudes changed little between the pre- and postintervention surveys. Although this may have been due to the timing of the surveys and to the fact that the changeover in personnel meant that almost an entirely different set of personnel responded to them, it is likely that the intervention did not affect some basic organization and work-design parameters significantly enough to boost attitudes beyond the already positive state in which they were originally found.

Analysis and Some Learnings from the Case

The complexity of the process and the theoretical issues that the project confronted go far beyond our description. There is little doubt that full STS redesign of the DPU was constrained by the larger military organization of which it was a part. Aspects of this case specifically relevant to military organizations are available elsewhere.[4] Here we include it to illustrate the use of a parallel learning structure for sociotechnical redesign in a highly rigid, traditional organization.[5]

The parallel learning structure aids in STS redesign in three fundamental ways, which we will explore in some detail. First, it provides a vehicle for organizational members to participate in a sociotechnical systems analysis of organizational needs and plan the redesign based on that analysis. Second, it can act as a transitional structure while the new design is being implemented. Third, and perhaps most important, the experience of participating in a parallel learning structure can teach people about the norms, roles, and procedures that are necessary for working in a jointly optimized system.

Parallel Learning Structure and STS Analysis

Using a parallel learning structure for doing STS analysis and redesign planning is practically the same as using a parallel learning structure for solving a messy problem or aiding an organization to adapt. The process isn't much different except that in this case there is one, specific framework for co-inquiry that may be foreign to organizational members. This creates a greater amount of dependence on outside expertise, maintains a power imbalance, and retards the process of groups' developing their own authority.

---

4. Pasmore, Shani, and Mietus (1982).

5. For those unfamiliar with this theory, information on sociotechnical systems can be found further in this chapter and in Appendix A of this book.

It is worth spending a moment recapturing the planned change process portrayed by this intervention at the DPU. In the first phase, the consultants performed an initial scan of the organization. Based on the results, they met with upper management and decided how best to proceed. A decision was reached to go ahead with a parallel learning structure as the mechanism for a full-fledged STS analysis. A parallel learning structure was formed, consisting of a steering committee and two study groups. They were handed a vision statement and strategy, which had been defined by the consultants and the director. Members of the parallel learning structure had little to do with the formation of these goals.

Following some basic education and training, the parallel learning structure proceeded to develop the data-collection tools and to identify the potential data sources within the organization. After the information was collected, the parallel learning structure had to digest the data, develop a shared perception of organizational reality, and identify potential changes using the STS design principles—all directed toward joint optimization. The parallel learning structure came up with several proposals, assessed them, and made recommendations to top management. Once several of the recommendations were accepted, the task became one of planning and executing implementation in such a way as to keep disruption of the unit's operation to a minimum.

An ongoing concern throughout the project was the group's dependency on both the consultants' STS expertise and the CO as the energy source for the project. The actual transformation of ownership of the project occurred during the process of data interpretation and development of recommendations. The high energy level generated by discussing ideas for change made it relatively easy for the internal consultant to let the groups take full responsibility for their process and decisions. By this point, the groups had acquired the basic group problem-solving skills and developed effective norms and working procedures. But it was not until the data were in and the groups went to work on creating "solutions" that members became personally committed to the process. As the two study groups merged into one with the CO as one of the group members, his energy and surprising degree of openness to new ideas were contagious, and the parallel structure was fired up to lead the organization's transformation.

Parallel Learning Structure as a Transitional Vehicle

One of the unintended outcomes of the project was the self-initiated transformation of the parallel learning structure into the transitional vehicle for implementing the redesign. As described in the case, when asked to develop suggestions for the physical design of the new space, the parallel structure proposed ideas that were complementary with their recommendations for STS redesign. When it came time to implement the changes, top management felt that they needed to call on the level of expertise and knowledge that had accumulated within the parallel structure.

At that point, the parallel learning structure went through a redesign itself. Structurally, it changed from four groups (steering committee, two study groups, and a consulting team) into two groups (steering committee and one study group). The structure's focus changed from studying organizational issues and recommending solutions to managing a complex organizational change. The co-inquiry and learning norms that had developed in the parallel structure enhanced smooth problem solving and decision making, but the power dynamics clearly changed with the CO's first-hand involvement. The first meeting of the modified parallel structure was devoted to integrating the new study group and defining the revised tasks and roles. The fact that the CO was perceived as an open-minded human being helped make this integration easier than it might have been.

Moving from being a learning structure to being an implementing structure was an easy transition for all members. No doubt, the role of accomplishing set goals was familiar to members. At this point, the parallel structure was, essentially, implementing a system-transforming innovation (Chapter 4), and a great part of its role was identifying and responding to problems and crises during the implementation itself. By applying the STS design principle of flexibly implementing and redesigning systems on the basis of actual user experience, the implementation progressed relatively smoothly Especially helpful was the parallel structure's ability to manage issues that spanned several boundaries or would normally "fall between the cracks." The quick implementation, and the fact that within six months the unit was performing at its highest levels ever, attest to the efficacy of this implementation strategy.

Parallel Learning Structure as a "Real-Time" Training Experience in STS Design

Pasmore (1988) has recently grouped STS design principles into six categories: (1) using social and technical resources effectively, (2) developing commitment and energy, (3) maximizing cooperative effort, (4) developing an awareness of the external environment, (5) developing human resources, and (6) sponsoring innovation rather than preserving the status quo. Many of these design attributes are based on normative assumptions and procedures quite different from those of traditional bureaucracies. Below we'll look at three specific elements of STS design theory that are in opposition to normal, bureaucratic design practice. As will become apparent, each of these STS design principles is implicit in parallel learning structures. Experience in parallel learning structures makes these contentious STS design principles seem less foreign and more acceptable to managers who are used to operating in traditional bureaucracies. By participating in a parallel learning structure, which is less risky than entering into a total redesign, they have a "real-time" training experience that enables them to envision the possibility of STS redesign.

A. Minimum Critical Specification.
This principle of STS design states that advance planning of work organization should specify only the very minimum needed to get it operating and then allow those who actually work in the system to elaborate their own procedures as learning takes place. This not only allows for greater involvement and ownership of employees over their work process, it also allows for "bottoms to optimize work processes" (Chapter 5) and ensures that options are not closed prematurely. Therefore, greater innovation and flexibility in handling unforeseen contingencies are possible.

This is at odds with traditional bureaucratic design, where experts are responsible for designing work processes and encouraged to make them "idiot proof." The last people invited to tinker with the designs are those who actually work inside them. This design principle, in which the total system is designed in advance against some ideal set of criteria in an attempt to eliminate as much uncertainty as possible, might be referred to as "total specification."

Parallel learning structures, however, operate under the normative assumptions of minimal critical specification. Their very existence implies that employees (not just experts) know something important about their work. They are designed to allow individual, creative contribution, not to guard against "idiots." Further, the parallel learning structure is loosely designed and open to self-modification on the basis of learning.

In the DPU case we see that top management was willing to relinquish some control to a diverse group of employees and flexibly implement a redesign. How likely would this be to happen in a military unit without the parallel learning structure experience?

B. Controlling Variance at Source. In STS terms, "variance" is any unprogrammed activity or unplanned-for event. Such occurrences are novelties, which require a decision and/or action. STS design principles call for controlling variance as close to the source of the variance as possible. In practical terms, this means that employees have decision-making authority over work in process.

This structure is totally at odds with traditional bureaucratic design. In bureaucratic design, the ideal is to ensure that all possible variances are already planned for. This means that in practice many variances go uncontrolled (e.g., mountains of scrap pile up in manufacturing) or variance is controlled many steps in the hierarchy away from where it is first noticed.

By giving managers the experience of relying on employees to make decisions in response to the novel and unexpected circumstances that arise, parallel learning structures accomplish two important things. First, they reinforce the effectiveness of employees controlling variance at its source, and second, they demonstrate that managers' fears associated with "giving up control" are exaggerated. By the end of the case, we see the shift in expectations during a major military exercise when the CO is required to make only one decision. It was not that there were no exceptions to manage; rather, those closest to the exceptions knew what was required and felt they had the authority to make the necessary decisions. Rather than feeling his authority was being usurped, the CO felt this was evidence of substantial, positive change in the unit.

C. Psychological Impact of Job Design. In traditional bureaucratic organizations, jobs continue to be designed in ways that are clearly psychologically impoverishing. At the operating level, tasks tend to be broken down into simple, repetitive actions. One person is given one job and is supervised by someone else. Decisions are made by authorities, and employees' attempts to innovate are usually discouraged.

One of the most visible features of many STS designs is the use of small groups of operating personnel to perform multiple tasks. The group is assigned a total set of operations that result in some identifiable, "whole task" and given the authority to accomplish the task as it sees fit. This greatly increases the opportunities for employees to tap sources of psychological fulfillment.[6] For example, they can acquire "skill variety" through internal rotation of jobs, "task identity" through having a recognizable output, "autonomy" through the group's decision-making authority, and "social interaction" through necessary interaction with other group members. Naturally, the institution of such "semiautonomous work groups" requires changing the roles of supervision and management away from controlling and toward coaching and facilitating.

The parallel learning structure provides an opportunity for managers to experience the real opportunities (and problems) of group-based organizational designs. Unlike the formal structure, the parallel structure involves groups grappling with whole tasks. Groups have the authority to create their own methods to accomplish the task, and decisions are made by consensus (not authority). Supervisors used to working in structures that engender employee dissatisfaction come to assume from experience that employees naturally dislike work and are primarily motivated by threats and money. The suggestion that they be allowed to manage themselves, and that this will be motivating, seems dubious to these supervisors. But by observing their employees in the parallel learning structure, they come to realize that many employees do want to be involved in their work and will be motivated by recognition and the chance to make a difference.

The DPU went to a group-based design. Because of the high levels of expertise required of operators in the DPU, it may be more difficult for the reader to imagine this shift taking place in the thinking of supervisors and managers, and attribute it to the parallel

---

6. For more on the psychological effects of job design, see Hackman and Oldham (1980).

learning structure. We have, however, observed this shift even in assembly-line manufacturing plants like the one in Chapter 5. In the DPU case, the use of semiautonomous project teams was clearly out of step with the traditional, hierarchically oriented, supervision-intensive style of military management.

In general, then, the parallel learning structure provides managers in traditionally structured bureaucracies an opportunity to observe and experience some of the underlying normative assumptions and procedures of STS designs that are the opposite of bureaucratic design (see Table 6.1). Rather than being told about the virtues of STS design, managers get to experience them without giving up the traditional structure they are used to. This is much less risky than agreeing to a redesign based on principles that don't fit one's own experience. Some other relevant learnings typically fostered by parallel structure membership include discovering that subordinates will act responsibly when given responsibility; that compliance occurs more readily under participative as opposed to directive leadership; that cohesive groups ensure compliance more effectively than rules do; that it is more effective to have those closest to the source of problems work on solving those problems; and that it is more effective to have boundaries between work units managed by members of those work units. Parallel structure membership is a "real-time training" event, and it allows for a cultural shift to begin without a massive, up-front commitment to implementing a design paradigm that is at odds with the daily experience of managers and supervisors in rigidly designed, formal bureaucracies.

Key Points in Using Parallel Learning Structures for Sociotechnical Systems Redesign

1. It is obviously vital that individuals trained in STS design be fully involved in the parallel structure. These individuals will likely have group facilitator roles.

2. Consider and use STS design principles whenever possible in designing the parallel learning structure. The parallel learning structure is an opportunity for real-time learning/training about STS. Use every opportunity to help managers link their experiences in the parallel learning structure to STS theory.

Table 6.1
Comparison of Normative Assumptions and Procedures Inherent in Rigid Bureaucracies and Parallel Learning Structures

Rigid Bureaucracy	Parallel Learning Structure
Normative Assumptions	
Subordinates naturally dislike and avoid work	Subordinates naturally want to be involved in their work and will volunteer for greater involvement
Subordinates are motivated through extrinsic threats and rewards	Subordinates are motivated through recognition and the opportunity to influence events
Make systems idiot proof	Make systems that allow for individual creative contribution
Subordinates should only be seen working and not heard	Subordinates should be encouraged to give ideas and opinions
There are experts for everything, and only they know what's important	Everyone knows something important about his or her work
Procedures	
Break down tasks into simple, repetitive actions	Grapple with whole tasks
One person, one job	Whole group, whole task
One person supervises many	Leadership emerges and is distributed throughout the group
Decisions are made by authorities	Decisions are made by group consensus
Enforce rules and standards	Question rules and standards
In Summary	
Manage people through tasks	Manage tasks through people

3. The role of the CEO in relation to the steering committee and the parallel learning structure needs to be carefully negotiated and renegotiated as the project progresses. In the DPU case, the CO renegotiated his role a few times: from detached CEO to steering committee member to member of the study team over a period of 18 months. Although the CEO's role may be an issue in any parallel structure application, it is critically important when the whole organization is being redesigned. Providing structure is a key task of tops in a system, and they must be fully involved in any implementation. If the CEO is a dominant personality, then the consultants should work closely with him or her to ensure that they help build a learning culture in the parallel structure and not overpower it.

4. There will be a push by all senior managers to be involved in the steering committee. If this happens, it is unlikely that the parallel learning structure will be able to develop a culture different from the operating organization. It is therefore important that not all top management be on the steering committee and that some members from other managerial levels be there instead.

5. Strive toward creating a parallel learning structure that is a microcosm of the organization. Avoid having one-third top management, one-third middle management, and one-third workers in the formation of the parallel structure. Workers are likely to perceive this kind of apportionment as two-thirds management and one-third workers, and in any case, it is not a true microcosm of the organization.

6. Because a specific theoretical base is being used for the analysis and redesign, there will be more dependence on the consultants than in other applications. While this is realistic at first, deliberate steps need to be taken to ensure that the parallel structure is operating in a co-inquiry mode by the data-interpretation phase or the output will be less than optimal.

7. Plan at the outset for the parallel *learning* structure to cease operations during implementation. Whether this means reforming the parallel structure or creating a new

vehicle for implementation is best left up to each unique organization to decide. There do, however, appear to be benefits to using a reformed parallel learning structure as the transition vehicle.

7

The Generic Intervention Model

This chapter presents a generic model of parallel learning structure formation and operation.[1] Here we will identify some of the basic phases in implementing a parallel learning structure as well as the key processes that need to be managed. As we progressed through our own learning and discoveries it became evident that parallel learning structures are used and can be used for very different purposes. In our experience, the espoused purpose, as identified by the organization during the initial client-consultant dialogue, influences the formation, the design, and the actual operation of the parallel structure.

Some organizations that find themselves bogged down by extensive layers of hierarchy have established parallel learning structures to open channels of communication. Other organizations faced with ill-defined problems (problems that involve more than just a few units in the organization, problems that don't necessarily have a "correct" solution, or problems that can never be fully resolved as they are always present) have created parallel structures as a mechanism to address challenges that the formal organization could not handle. Organizations that require flexibility and innovation, yet face the efficiency demands of a competitive industry, find that parallel learning structures help solve the complex problems resulting from such conflicting motivations. Parallel learning structures

---

1. Thanks to Dan Wise for his help in developing this model.

have been used to assist the process of system transformation and organizational change along the lines of sociotechnical systems theory, as well as in the implementation of complex, system-wide innovations. Unionized organizations have found parallel learning structures useful in improving labor-management relations and developing jointly sponsored change projects.

We have found that the unique characteristics of each organization, coupled with the unique demands of each purpose, lead to the creation of distinct parallel learning structures in most cases. And so it should be. Interventions should be tailored to meet the needs of each system. Yet, in spite of the distinct characteristics of each parallel learning structure we have seen, there are some basic similarities in the processes involved in their creation and operation. Out of an appreciation of those similarities, we have developed a generic model to guide these interventions. The purpose of this chapter is to introduce that model. The model is, by its general nature, somewhat simplified and therefore limited. Nonetheless, the model can be used by managers and organization development practitioners as a cognitive map and a guide when considering the introduction of a parallel learning structure into an organization. It is important to keep in mind that parallel learning structures are neither a quick fix nor a cosmetic change. A parallel learning structure intervention is an involved effort that requires managerial commitment, readiness to allocate resources, openness to examination of current organization practices, operations, and policies, and willingness to experiment and learn. If followed as outlined in our model, the intervention can last anywhere from several months to several years.

An Overview of the Parallel Learning Structure Intervention Model

Parallel learning structure interventions, like most technostructural interventions, are complex and require the whole array of organization development skills. As indicated in Table 7.1, there are eight phases in the change model.

Phase 1: Initial Definition of Purpose and Scope

The first phase in the intervention is similar to any initial scouting and entry sequence. Because of the system-wide nature of the

Table 7.1
The Generic Parallel Learning Structure Intervention Process

Phase 1:	Initial Definition of Purpose and Scope
Phase 2:	Formation of a Steering Committee
	2.1 Re-examining the need for change
	2.2 Creating a vision statement
	2.3 Defining boundaries, strategies, expectations, and rewards
Phase 3:	Communicating to Organization Members
Phase 4:	Formation and Development of Study Groups
	4.1 Selecting and developing internal facilitators
	4.2 Selecting study group members
	4.3 Study group development
	4.4 Establishing working procedures and norms
Phase 5:	The Inquiry Process
Phase 6:	Identifying Potential Changes
Phase 7:	Experimental Implementation of Proposed Changes
Phase 8:	System-wide Diffusion and Evaluation

intervention, the initial client contact is almost always a senior executive (though sometimes it may be an internal consultant who is working with senior managers). Sometimes a parallel learning structure intervention is recommended after an extensive study of the organization. In any event, some organizational scanning and assessment leads to the conclusion that a parallel learning structure will respond to the organization's felt need. At this point, there is some need to educate key decision makers about parallel learning structure interventions and the commitment they require. An initial discussion of potential roles, activities, outcomes, and costs is necessary, as well as an understanding that flexibility is needed to redefine these things as the organization learns. Some are set up to work on specific problems within finite time limits. Those limits should be clearly specified and delineated within this phase. Other parallel learning structures are created with indefinite time boundaries to function in an ongoing manner. In either case, the senior management group should have a clear sense of the purpose of the intervention and their expectations for how the parallel learning structure will function and should be able to articulate those purposes and expectations to others in the organization.

Phase 2: Formation of a Steering Committee

All parallel learning structures require a steering committee, usually made up of a cross-section of top-level decision makers in the organization. The steering committee has as a minimum the following roles:

1. to further define the purpose and scope of the project
2. to develop a vision statement for the effort
3. to guide the creation and implementation of the parallel learning structure
4. to establish the linkage mechanisms between the parallel learning structure and the formal organization
5. to sanction the activities of the parallel learning structure
6. to ensure the support of senior management

It is important that this committee have and be perceived as having the authority to sanction the actions of the parallel learning structure. We cannot overemphasize the importance of having a high level of commitment by the steering committee to the *purpose* for which the parallel learning structure is formed, if not for the parallel learning structure itself.

The steering committee may be made up of individuals with diverse personalities, responsibilities, and constituencies. In fact, it is important that it include individuals who have the respect of, and are considered the leaders of, the various factions within the organization. In a unionized organization, the steering committee may consist of both top-level managers and their union counterparts. In a hospital, the committee would likely include members of the medical and nursing staffs, as well as administrative personnel. Those at the top of the organization(s) are the key decision makers in creating the steering committee and deciding upon its membership.

2.1 Re-examining the Need for Change

The OD practitioner plays an important role in the formation of the steering committee. A key challenge at this phase is to establish a climate for learning and innovation. This requires using a co-inquiry process that reduces dependence on authority or expertise for learning and, instead, emphasizes that everyone has resources to contribute to the understanding and resolution of organizational problems. The OD practitioner is likely to find himself or herself in the position of having to educate the steering committee despite predictable skepticism. At this point, clear emphasis on the task of establishing shared agreement on the purpose of the intervention is an important first step. Since the steering committee will determine the scope and boundaries for the functioning of the parallel learning structure, it is important for the committee to evaluate both the internal and external forces stimulating change. Various organization development techniques, like open-systems planning, force-field analysis, and intergroup mirroring can be used to accomplish this. It is very important in this phase to model good parallel learning structure working procedures and norms and to manage conflicts constructively.

2.2 Creating a Vision Statement

One of the outcomes of this co-inquiry into the need for change should be a specific vision-statement document. Such a statement can include information about where the organization is, where it is expected to be, and how the implementation of a parallel learning structure will help it get there. This vision statement will later be shared with the study groups. It can be further refined by the study groups. Having study groups refine the statement is especially useful in a system characterized by fear and distrust as it increases ownership of the process. Once approved by the top management of the formal organization, the vision statement should be conveyed to the organization as a whole. The clarity of this vision appears to have implications for the success of the intervention, though experiences vary greatly.

2.3 Defining Boundaries, Strategies, Expectations, and Rewards

For the parallel learning structure to function effectively, its purpose must be sufficiently defined. The steering committee should delineate the initial set of activities for the parallel structure to work on. To do so, they must take a look at the overall organization and its functioning and come to a consensus as to the priority problem areas.

The task-definition statement coming out of the steering committee will necessarily be broad. A health care institution might set a goal of improving medical staff-administration relations. A military organization may choose to focus on absenteeism and morale problems. An industrial firm might choose to look at problems with product quality. Since the strength of the parallel learning structure is its ability to respond to an organizational need that the formal organization is unable to address, it is important at this stage of the intervention to keep the focus broad but manageable.

The steering committee also creates the procedures and criteria for the formation and operation of the study groups within the parallel learning structure. The steering committee should consider exactly how the groups will be constituted, and it may want to consider what rewards exist (or could be created) for the participation of organizational members in the study groups. Furthermore, the steering committee might want to determine appropriate measurements and dimensions for assessing the progress and the success of the parallel learning structure activities.

In many applications, formation of the parallel learning structure requires the use of internal facilitators with specialized knowledge. What is needed may simply be group facilitation skills, or it may be special analytical procedures. Prior to implementation, the steering committee has to address whether such facilitation is necessary, and if so, whether individuals with the skills to be facilitators already exist or must be trained.

Phase 3: Communicating to Organization Members

One of the characteristics of parallel learning structures is a high level of organizational participation in the change process. In order for this to occur, it is important for all members of the organization to remain informed about the intervention activities. Organization members are usually informed about the intervention for the first time at the end of the first phase through a public announcement by the CEO.

The primary thrust of communication is likely to occur after the creation of the vision statement at the end of the second phase. At this point, the vision is shared throughout the organization. Additionally, employees are invited to assemblies or other information forums where the main purposes of the intervention, the mechanisms, the projected lifetime, the phases and initial activities, the need for involvement, and the potential benefits of the parallel learning structure are shared. Managers can share the vision determined by the steering committee and ask for initial input and feedback from organizational members. The purpose of this information sharing is twofold. First, informed members might feel more comfortable with the process. Second, those organization members who are particularly interested in the process will make themselves known during these sessions. These individuals might be potential candidates for the study groups.

Where there is a great need to keep everyone informed of the parallel learning structure's activities, publication and distribution of minutes from meetings has been used with some success.

Phase 4: Formation and Development of Study Groups

The formation of the study groups involves selecting and training internal facilitators, establishing of criteria and selecting learning group members, developing effective groups, and establishing clear boundaries around the parallel learning structure.

4.1 Selecting and Training Internal Facilitators

The internal group facilitators can play a critical role in making the study groups work effectively. If organizational members are used to working in groups without appointed leaders, facilitators may not be necessary. In a lot of cases, however, the success or failure of the entire effort rests on the facilitators' ability and skills. We have found that by identifying the group facilitators and by providing them with some basic group facilitation skills prior to the first meeting of the study groups, the parallel structure has been more effective and satisfying for group members. Group facilitators are charged with the responsibility for developing the internal climate necessary for co-inquiry, learning, and creativity. They need to have some skill at process consultation.[2] They give early direction to the study groups for dealing with the tasks at hand. As the groups mature and

---

2. Schein (1988).

accomplish tasks successfully, some have chosen to rotate the facilitator role among group members. The rotation norm provides individual members with the opportunity to learn a new set of skills and reinforces the sense of equal responsibility for the group's outcomes.

Individuals are selected from the organization by criteria established by the steering committee. Such criteria might include their visibility within the organization, their skills at working with people and working with groups, and their desire to act in this role. Once selected, internal facilitators receive basic training (if they aren't already skilled) in group dynamics, communication, conflict resolution, group problem solving, decision making and team building. They go through exercises designed to increase trust and break down barriers to communication. They also learn a little about parallel learning structures, action research, and organizational change and development. The facilitators play a critical role in conveying and facilitating some of this understanding to the study group members.

4.2 Selecting Study Group Members

Study group membership can be determined in several ways. We have found that some combination of volunteers and appointees creates well-balanced groups. Managers can be asked to recommend individuals that they feel "fit the bill." All organizational members can be invited to sign up for a group during the information-sharing session in Phase 3. The degree to which individuals choose to be involved has a lot to do with the organizational culture and past experiences. It can be expected that in the early stages of the parallel learning structure, there may be some reluctance to participate. This is especially true where there have been strained relations between management and the work force and/or past experiences of raised expectations that weren't met. These reservations are usually overcome after management's sincerity has been tested in some way and/or an influential member of the work force becomes committed to the process. Honesty and openness with information about the project helps in these situations. The steering committee usually makes the final decisions regarding learning group membership based on criteria it has established and made known. It is important that this selection process is not perceived as playing favorites or in any way construed as an attempt to white-wash the issues. In other words, employees must feel well represented in the study groups and trust the process by which the members were selected.

Study groups may include members of the steering committee. These dual memberships become liaisons that can play a critical role in facilitating the communication between the study groups and the steering committee. The study groups are comprised of members from various levels of the organization. Depending on the size and structure of the organization, there may be individuals from each hierarchical level, or various groups may be formed in different divisions and at different levels. The latter design depends on a "cascade" effect, wherein the parallel learning structure is implemented at first at higher levels of management and cascades down to each of the work areas and levels.

While parallel group membership should be representative of the whole organization, it is important that members not be "official" representatives of any group. Being an official representative creates psychological pressure to represent the group's interests, which reduces individual initiative and makes it more difficult to take the organization's interests as a whole into account. It also increases the intergroup dynamics at play in the study group and makes them more difficult to resolve within the group.

4.3 Study Group Development

One of the unique aspects of parallel learning structures is the disposal of the formal lines of hierarchy within the study groups. Each member is an equal with all other members. However, it will take strenuous effort on the part of the OD professional and the internal facilitator to bring the group to this level of communication and trust.

The first efforts within the study groups should be to open the channels of communication between members. Sharing of the overall vision and purpose of the "experiment" is an important start. Soliciting the group's response to this vision and suggestions on how to go about achieving it are likewise important. Typical team-building activities are appropriate at this stage. Even more important than the team building itself is the need to overcome individuals' reticence in talking to superiors. It is important that everyone in the group feel willing to share his or her input. It is often necessary to counsel individuals who are managers in the formal hierarchy to make them understand the potential dampening effect of authority dynamics. Rotating responsibility for chairing meetings may also help equalize the leadership of the meetings.

In organizations with highly differentiated subgroups, typical intergroup dynamics are likely to play out. Members will begin by treating each other as representatives of these different groups, and you can expect a certain amount of stereotyping. Members will have to get past these stereotypes and develop an appreciation for each other as individuals before they can build an effective group.

4.4 Establishing Working Procedures and Norms

Part of the team-building effort is establishing the norms and procedures that will be used within the study groups, between the study groups, and between the study groups and the steering committee. These norms include such things as when the groups are to meet, what they will accomplish, how the meetings will be organized, what kinds of roles are needed in order for the group to function optimally, how they will assess their effectiveness, how they should relate to each other and to the steering committee, and what their relationship is to their "constituencies." We have found that the communication procedures between the study groups and the steering committee, and between the groups and the organization members at large, are critical to the success of any parallel learning structure effort. Group participation in establishing these procedures and norms is important. The implementation of the procedures should be perceived as experimental and to be further refined as the groups work with them and examine their effectiveness and performance. In general, those processes and procedures that support synergistic, group problem solving are the ones to be encouraged.

Phase 5: The Inquiry Process

It is difficult to generalize this phase across all the different parallel learning structure interventions we're familiar with. Different purposes lead to different inquiry strategies. Generically speaking, this phase involves a co-inquiry process by the study group(s) around a clearly defined issue(s). A joint exploration of different inquiry methods and their degree of fit to the organization and the problem(s) at hand, the actual data-collection procedures, analysis of the data, and the collective attempt to construct shared meaning from the data are all potential steps and activities during this phase. It is important to note, however, that this phase varies significantly from one parallel learning structure intervention to another in the degree of analytical rigor that is employed. While some interventions choose to use action-research methods, others might follow a pure problem-solving approach, while still others might use empirical, scientific methods. In some cases, data collection and analysis really consist of people talking to each other in ways they normally don't.

The role of the OD practitioner is to guide the steering committee and the study group(s) in these decisions, to provide information about the advantages and disadvantages of each method, and to be a part of the co-inquiry process. Aside from the content of the inquiry, part of the facilitation of the co-inquiry processes requires a respect for the nature of "tacit knowledge" and an ability to aid people in articulating what they "know" but don't know how to say. Another aspect of co-inquiry relates to knowledge that people have but are unwilling to articulate. Generally, this happens when people are afraid of repercussions that might occur by saying something. Therefore, co-inquiry and the emergence of explicit knowledge are aided by developing norms that encourage a learning orientation, basic trust despite status differentials, the expression of half thoughts and fuzzy ideas, and the expression of potentially conflict-producing ideas.

The collective attempt to develop shared understanding and meaning from the data is an elaborate and complex process. The steering committee and the study group(s) bring together parties whose personal objectives, inquiry goals, inquiry methods, percep-tions, and conceptual and practical frameworks are often different. The failure to integrate diversity can result in ambiguity, conflict, confusion, and, at times, a sense of hopelessness. This is the risk. On the other hand, successful integration and development of common understanding is a source of joy and development that unleashes tremendous productive and healing energy.

Phase 6: Identifying Potential Changes

Based on the information gathered and the development of shared meaning of the data collected, the study groups can begin the process of devising potential solutions and actions. During this phase, the ongoing dialogue and sharing of ideas between study group members and members of the organization at large can be vital. Ideally, clear and effective communication procedures between the parallel learning structure and others in the organization have now been established and information flows quickly. The role of the facilitator at this stage is to facilitate group creativity and establish effective problem-solving procedures.

The net result of this is often a proposal for change that gets sent to the steering committee for approval and implementation. In permanent parallel learning structures, however, groups are often encouraged to implement their own ideas without steering committee approval in situations where implementation would have minor resource implications and would not affect the work of many others. The steering committee should create and update guidelines for how proposals should be presented and what kind of information should be included (e.g., data analysis, alternative solutions, cost-benefit analysis).

Phase 7: Experimental Implementation of Proposed Changes

This phase of the intervention consists of experimental implementation of the recommendations proposed by the parallel learning structure. Procedurally, before any major change can be implemented, the proposal must receive steering committee and management approval. The presence of a steering committee member in the study group can greatly facilitate the review process, as the steering committee will have a member knowledgeable about the background that led to the specific proposal. It is important, too, that proposals coming from the study groups be thoroughly reviewed by the steering committee against a set of criteria. The steering committee should provide detailed feedback to the study groups on each proposal. Once the proposal is endorsed by the steering committee, in most cases it has to be presented and approved by the top management of the formal organization. To the extent that top-level management of the organization is informed on a continuous basis about the activities and the progress made by the parallel learning structure, the reactions to the ideas generated by the parallel learning structure are more positive. In many cases, the perceived seriousness of the response of upper management is interpreted by study group members as the commitment of upper management to the effort as a whole.

Proposals that merely call for the purchase or installation of a new piece of equipment or a relatively minor change in a work flow do not require much experimentation. Once they are approved, their execution is quite simple and may be carried out without much difficulty through the formal organization's procedures. The more system-wide the implications of the proposed ideas, however, the greater the need for experimental implementation prior to a system-wide diffusion. Once the proposal is approved, the necessary resources allocated, the boundaries for the experiment set, and the assessment measures delineated, it is senior management's responsibility to carry out the experimental implementation. In some cases, the parallel learning structure might be asked to take responsibility and lead the implementation. In other cases, senior management may delegate the task to other organizational members or organizational units. In any case, final responsibility for the experiment must be in senior management's hands. An assessment of the experimental implementation will almost always result in some modifications of the ideas and the methods used to implement them. The experiment will also aid in planning for and managing organization-wide implementation.

The entire parallel learning structure intervention process can be viewed as experimental; that is, all decisions, mechanisms, processes, commitments, and outcomes are open for modification based on trial-and-error learning. As such, experimentation can be viewed as an overarching value above and beyond the intervention— that's why this is a *learning* structure. Therefore, parallel learning structure interventions require the company's commitment to allow experiments to operate without pressure for premature performance. Failures that produce learning must be accepted.

Phase 8: System-wide Diffusion and Evaluation

Part of the implementation process is the ongoing experimental implementation and evaluation of the effectiveness of the change. Organizations vary in the approach taken for system-wide diffusion of ideas and management of change. The learning from the experimental implementation phase usually provides decision makers with clues about the potential roadblocks and challenges inherent in the change and helps in the planning and actual managing of the system-wide implementation process. The diffusion and evaluation of the changes requires thoughtful planning and skillful managing. The failure to diffuse an innovative idea system-wide will threaten the long-term durability of the parallel learning structure. Not providing the organization with an accurate assessment of the effort will prevent the organization in general and the parallel learning structure in particular from acquiring valuable, and potentially crucial, information and knowledge.

Conducting a valid assessment of change, particularly large system change, is an art still under development. On the one hand, we have debates among researchers about the meaning of "valid scientific research," "threats to validity," and limitations of empirical methods in social systems. On the other hand, few managers and consultants have a taste for research. Most managers are content to assess the effectiveness of changes by gut feel. Unfortunately, if the assessment of change is not managed properly, it can not only produce misleading information but can reduce people's trust in the change process as well. It is important that the parallel learning structure take seriously the need to provide a mechanism for a valid assessment. We have found the very best approach to be the involvement of a group of skilled, unbiased, external researchers who initially work closely with the parallel learning structure and then put together their scientific assessment. This approach has been very beneficial both to the organizations involved and the academic community. Results of such evaluations are usually fed back to the parallel learning structure. The steering committee can then redefine its vision statement and/or the boundaries and redirect the parallel learning structure's activities.

A Final Caveat

The model presented in this chapter is an overview of a general road map. The very simplicity of the model described might be its greatest drawback. As the cases demonstrate, no two organizations are alike, nor are any two organizational needs or problems identical. Business situations are always more complex than the simplicity of this model implies. Factors and personalities outside of the "traditional" model will almost certainly be present to complicate the dynamics. Personality conflicts, managers and/or union leaders refusing to relinquish power, and decision makers deciding they are unwilling to commit resources to solve problems are fairly typical challenges those trying to create parallel learning structures face.

There are drawbacks to the use of parallel learning structures that are similar to most technostructural interventions. The most important ones are, of course, the time and resource requirements involved. It takes a significant amount of time and commitment to develop the necessary level of trust and communication within the parallel learning structure and between the parallel learning structure and the formal organization. It also takes multiple skills and patience on the part of the practitioner. A minimum of a few months is required to plan and manage the creation of the parallel learning structure and establish its norms and working procedures. During this time, virtually no outcome is visible. Furthermore, there may be some disturbance in overall organizational performance. Nevertheless, once a climate of co-inquiry is established and members buy into the authenticity of the parallel learning structure, they are almost always willing to commit to full-scale learning, experimenting, and doing what is needed to create the kind of organization they want to work in.

Parallel learning structure interventions almost always result in changes in an organization. It is important to note, however, that there are many other forces—environmental, economic, cognitive, and attitudinal—that not only foster their own changes, but have a significant effect on the learning process. Many of these forces are contextual and might have little or a lot to do with the intervention at each phase of its development. These other forces might alter the parallel structure's direction, its process, and/or its outcomes. For this model to be helpful, don't follow it blindly and dogmatically. The goal should be to help the organization establish a structure for inquiry, experimentation, and learning that will be the most appropriate for its needs.

In the following chapter, we turn to theoretical issues of organizational learning and change. Specific techniques and interventions must be driven by theory so that they can be customized to fit the needs of the system. Technique (know-how) without theory (know-why) seldom produces optimal results.

8

Organizational Learning and Metaphors of Change

In Chapters 2–6 we have seen that the unique characteristics of each organization, coupled with the unique demands of each purpose, result in uniquely designed parallel learning structures. At the end of each case, we described some of what we learned from the case and offered some theoretical guidelines and models for managing those distinct purposes. This chapter is a more general extension of our learnings. Its purpose is to expand the change agent's way of thinking about learning and change in organizations. We begin by reviewing blocks to learning in organizations and things that managers and consultants can do to increase learning. We then go on to look at different metaphors of change processes and the very different perspectives each one gives to the manager and consultant guiding the implementation of a parallel learning structure.

Blocks to Learning in Organizations

Since the purpose of parallel learning structures is to provide a space and time for learning to occur, it is useful to consider what typically blocks learning in organizations and pay attention to opportunities to overcome these blocks. The core consulting method that we have found to be of help for promoting learning in client systems is creating processes of *mutual,* or *"co"-inquiry.* Co-inquiry, similar to "action research" and "process consultation," means that organizational members, consultants, and maybe even clients *inquire together* into the issues the organization is facing and develop a common understanding of what the issues are and how to solve them.

To do this, consultants have to understand how learning occurs, what the blocks to learning in organizations are, and how to structure the consulting relationship to promote learning.

A Simple Model of How Learning Occurs

People learn in many different ways, but mostly they learn from experience. Experiential learning occurs when individuals pay attention and reflect on their experience, develop some generalizable notions or propositions that are different from their previous notions, and then experiment with or "act on" these new generalizations to see what happens. This "experiential learning cycle" is depicted in Fig. 8.1.[1]

The blocks to learning in organizations can mainly be found at the boundaries between each of these four moments in the learning cycle. Experiences that result in reflection are usually the unexpected or unwanted ones, things that we find surprising, puzzling, different from what we expected, or failures. In order to promote learning in organizations, people need to have clear expectations so they can see deviations. They need to have accurate information and timely feedback about the results of their actions. Without these, they are less likely to be stimulated to reflect. Therefore, it is important to help members clarify their expectations, generate accurate information, and put feedback loops into place.

Learning in organizations requires that people share their different points of view on experiences (group reflection) and develop common understandings about what can be generalized. It may be the very act of *group* reflection and generalization that distinguishes organizational learning from individual learning. Because the movement from reflection to generalization in group settings is blocked when people are afraid or unable to voice differences of perception and opinion, it is important to help members increase their appreciation and ability to tolerate differences. They must be able to have open conflict around ideas and believe that it is worth the time it takes to come to shared understandings.

More than this, however, is required: for learning to lock in, there has to be some action taken on these new understandings. The boundary between actions and the experience of those actions must

---

1. Kolb (1984).

Figure 8.1
The Experiential Learning Cycle

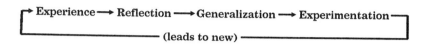

be managed to promote organizational learning. This requires a willingness to let go of what is well known and experiment with what has only been speculation. It is therefore important to help members find ways to test out new ideas in small ways, to define experiments as experiments, and not create premature pressures for "success."

Clarifying expectations, generating accurate information, putting feedback loops into place, sharing different points of view, taking time to develop common understandings, and protecting experiments from pressures for success are all useful for promoting learning in organizations. But they can all be difficult to do in organizations. Why?

A. Clarifying Expectations

Expectations play a critical role in any learning and organization development process.[2] Contracts, standards, requirements, and objectives are all forms of organizational expectations. If they change frequently with little notice or rationale, people stop paying attention to them. When people are consistently held accountable for expectations that they really have no control over, they tend to shy away from formulating clear expectations or work at formulating expectations that are low enough that they can be met easily. When expectations are consistently beyond what the organization is able to do and the organization continues operating without much visible change, people come to ignore expectations or develop a set of informal expectations.

Part of the "drama" of business is the formulation and monitoring of contracts, objectives, requirements, and standards.

---

2. Dov Eden's (1988) discussion of OD, productivity, and self-fulfilling prophecy in OD is worthwhile reading.

People can become very good at *appearing* to buy into expectations and then ignoring them. If you find that you are having problems getting groups in the parallel learning structure to formulate clear expectations and then act as if they believe them, check out whether there is a history of one or more of the problems described in the previous paragraph. If there is, try to get the group to talk about this history and what the disadvantages are of continuing to operate in this way.

The biggest problem with expectations in organizational change projects, however, is that few people are able to imagine things that they haven't already experienced. (We saw this especially at Triburg Manufacturing.) Managers who have never seen a plant at full capacity meet schedule, never seen on-time new product introduction, never seen cooperative intergroup meetings, or never seen whatever the change expectation is, probably will not really believe that it is possible. They may (on the off chance that it can happen) verbally agree to an expectation a consultant is pushing, but as long as they don't really believe the expectation, failure to meet it will not trigger learning. Prior learning can be the biggest impediment to future learning because people don't expect things to be any different. One of the best strategies for overcoming this problem is to send members off to look at places where those "wild, unrealistic expectations" are actually being met. It is well worth your time to cultivate relationships with organizations where things are being done "right" that will allow your clients or employees to visit and see for themselves.

B. Generating Accurate Information

Getting accurate information flowing between people, groups, and levels can be the biggest impediment to learning in organizations. This is one very big advantage of the parallel learning structure; it is designed to get information flowing between levels and groups. Sometimes the problem is a lack of means for generating accurate information. If you have the expertise, or know where to get it, this is a fairly easy problem to deal with once it is recognized. Much more difficult to deal with, and more prevalent, are distortions in information flows caused by distrust and fear. There are many ways such distrust and fear can be generated—for example, when "killing the messenger" is often observed; when people are consistently punished for failing to meet expectations, regardless of their past track records or unique circumstances; or when two or more groups are in competition for scarce resources.

Attempts to change such situations run into a "double whammy." To begin with, change agents must contend with the fears that created the distortions in the first place (like at Pittown Assembly and the Military Data Processing Unit). In addition, generating accurate information now would uncover past sins of omission and falsehoods that were committed "to make the numbers look right" (like at Triburg Manufacturing).

A lot of OD techniques are precisely designed to deal with such situations, probably because they are prevalent and because no one technique works all the time. What does work (if anything will) is to get the leaders of the organization talking together about problems with information flow, realistically examining its impact on their effectiveness, and making a commitment to change. We have found it useful to have those who are distorting information (usually at the lower levels) recommend ways of making it safer to pass on "bad news." When implementing new, more accurate information systems, it may be necessary to have some kind of "unconditional pardon" for past inaccurate information, but again, members of the parallel learning structure will know what needs to be done if you can start a process of co-inquiry.

Certain properties of hierarchical systems make it unlikely that distortion between levels can ever be fully eliminated. These are the positional dilemmas discussed in Chapter 5. Understanding these, however, will help you work around them.

C. Putting Feedback Loops into Place

Probably the biggest problem with creating feedback loops that allow people to learn how they are doing is that most information systems are designed for control and evaluation, not learning. This has two results. One is that information goes to the people doing the controlling and evaluating, not those doing the work. Obviously, the people doing the work are not going to be able to learn much without timely feedback on results. The advent of computer networks has made resolution of this problem fairly simple. The same information can easily be sent to both those doing the work and those doing the controlling. The second result is that much of the information collected in organizations is not that useful for learning purposes. The information will tell you that you haven't met expectations, but rarely will it help you figure out why. This seems to be a much more difficult problem to resolve. Collecting information can be costly, but those who control information collection need to look at the costs of not providing information that is useful for learning.

In large organizations, many important feedback loops are missing because they cross a number of internal boundaries and those with authority over all the different units are so far away from the problems that they may not even know problems exist. (As we saw, this was a problem in all the cases, especially Intercon.) Discovering what important feedback loops are missing is usually nine-tenths of the problem. Parallel learning structures that combine organizational units within the study groups often can readily clarify where information loops are missing and what would remedy the problem. Putting feedback loops into place is relatively easy (as long as there aren't forces at work to systematically distort information in the loops).

D. Sharing Different Points of View

Good reflection requires looking at an experience from as many different points of view as possible. Yet, in some organizations it is very difficult to get people to express unconventional perspectives publicly. (As was discovered at Pittown Assembly and at the Military Data Processing Unit.) Sometimes, this block to learning is an individual trait and sometimes it is created by the organization. Most people fear ridicule and embarrassment, and these fears can keep individuals from expressing very different points of view. About all you can do in such cases is support a person in taking a risk and seeing what happens (trying to make sure that the person won't be ridiculed when he or she does it).

When a lot of people in the organization won't speak up, there is something going on in the system. A senior manager who won't tolerate differences of opinion can close a lot of people down. There may be a history of people who weren't "team players" being shipped off to obscure posts. It may have been so long since anything new was listened to or tried that people have simply stopped thinking or speaking up (like at Grate Hospital).

In such systems, parallel learning structures can be thought of as attempts to revive constructive controversy. The fact that they are being tried means that senior managers feel a need to involve more employees and gain their perspectives on things. Employees, however, are unlikely to believe that things have changed. Initial study group meetings are likely to have an air of passive aggression. Typically, group members try an initial test to see if they get any response. This often takes the form of an innocuous request for information or action, of a type that is usually ignored. This is a critical point, and the steering committee must be ready to respond to such tests positively. Only then will members feel that they really can make a difference and be willing to put in the hard work that constructive controversy entails.

E. Taking Time to Develop Common Understandings

Developing truly shared understandings takes time, and time is a precious commodity in most businesses. Unless people have a common understanding of what the expectations are, what unexpected events could mean, how problems are being defined, and what experiments are trying to discover, organizational learning is retarded. Obviously, organizations cannot afford the time to ensure common understanding on all matters. This becomes a block to learning when managers are unwilling to take the time to arrive at common understanding on any issue. A useful intervention might be to get the parallel structure to look at what the costs have been in the past for assuming common understanding when none existed.

In general, there are two issues here. One may be that people are unskilled at communicating with each other, and developing common understanding takes more time and effort than is necessary. Using trained facilitators in the parallel learning structure is most important in such cases. Lack of ability can be overcome with practice and persistence.

The second issue is knowing what the really important things are; that is, where the benefits of taking the time will outweigh the costs. This is something that the parallel learning structure can inquire into for itself. By and large, common understanding is most important (from a learning perspective) for basic objectives (expectations) of the organization and when core operating assumptions (ways of accomplishing expectations) are being challenged and/or modified.

F. Protecting Experiments from Pressures for Success

All change and innovation is, to some extent, a step into the unknown. During a large change it is most important for organizations to be learning and taking corrective action based on experience. Sometimes, however, pressures are placed on innovators to "be successful" right from the start. This can lead to false reports of success and good money being thrown after bad. Organizations that have a high bias toward performance and a low appreciation of learning from errors can be particularly guilty of this. In such cases, promoting organizational learning is best done at the front end, before the experiment begins. As a consultant, it is a wise idea to ask around and find out what the pattern of innovation has been in the past. If the organization has a history of flogging dead horses, open this up as a subject for inquiry in the parallel learning structure. What has happened in the past and why? What can be done in the future to avoid situations worth avoiding?

There are a couple of things that can usually help ease premature pressures for success. One is simply to have innovations defined as experiments and plan to implement them on a limited, trial basis at first. Another is to help the client avoid situations where one individual or group is heavily associated with the innovation. Try to make innovations everyone's responsibility.

General Rules of Thumb

You can't force people to learn. If a lot of individuals in the organization are indifferent or hostile toward the organization, they probably aren't interested in putting in the effort that learning takes. A first diagnostic step in entering a client system is to find out to what extent employees are concerned about the organization and want to do a good job. If they don't care, remedial work needs to be done before you can make much headway in improving the organization's learning capacity. Organizations that are poor at learning need the most help and probably know it the least. If they knew it, they wouldn't be so poor at learning. In such cases, you need to spend a lot of up-front time clarifying the possibilities and limitations of parallel learning structure operation. Initially, the parallel learning structure will be working on developing a climate for cooperation and co-inquiry. Not much effort will go into solving messy problems or innovating, and senior management and the steering committee must recognize that. In such circumstances, parallel learning structure operation might best be seen as a two phased effort; first cleaning up the internal morale problems, then moving on to improving organizational output.

In suggesting a parallel learning structure intervention to a client, you are suggesting that the organization develop the capacity to identify and solve its own problems. Managers generally like to hear that you believe that all situations are unique and that you are not there to apply some "fix." They like to hear that you want to build capacity in their systems and not create dependence on you. They like to hear that your goal is to help them create a system of ongoing improvement. They may not like to hear that this will take time, require their effort and support, require they confront their own role in reducing learning and involve a lot of their managers in meetings, but they need to agree to that, too. Generally speaking, we have found that the more experience a manager has with consultants, the more likely he or she is to appreciate this approach.

Finally, pay attention to modeling good learning behavior in your interactions with the client system. Clarify expectations, generate accurate information, put feedback loops into place, share different points of view, take time to develop common understandings, and protect experiments from premature pressures for success.

Metaphors of Change

In this section, we'll look at the processes created and supported by parallel learning structures that generate learning and change in bureaucratic organizations. We'll briefly describe seven points of view, or "metaphors," of organizational change. We call them metaphors because, for the most part, they are processes humans have observed in nature, in individuals, and in societies. They are more like ways of looking at things than complete theories of how learning and change takes place in organizations. Some of them are highly speculative. Individually, none fully captures the process by which a parallel learning structure transforms an organization. Taken together or in combinations, however, they seem to provide satisfying explanations for changes we have observed in organizations using this intervention. The seven metaphors are the rational-brain, intrapreneurial, morphogenic, political, cell-mutation, morphic resonance, and chaos metaphors. We'll look at how each metaphor would explain the change process created by a parallel learning structure, and then go on to re-examine the cases in Chapters 2–6 from these different perspectives.

The Rational-Brain Metaphor

From this point of view, organizations are rational, goal-directed entities made up of rational, goal-oriented people who make decisions and take actions on the basis of the information they have. The parallel learning structure creates change because of the work done by people in the parallel structure. Thoughtful and committed people in well-run groups identify problems and opportunities for improvement. Groups are effectively linked to the formal organization, their ideas are funneled back into the formal organization, and the good ones are implemented.

The Intrapreneurial Metaphor

Organizations are collections of individuals with more or less knowledge, more or less motivation, and more or less access to resources necessary for effective performance. From this point of view, the most effective organizations are those that have knowledgeable, committed people who have access to the resources needed to perform their responsibilities and who constantly seek ways of improving themselves and the organization.

In organizations where there has been a history of lack of motivation for improvement and lack of access to resources for innovation, the parallel learning structure creates change because it provides a climate and structure that encourages individual and group initiative. The empowerment people experience provides the motivation and the networking opportunities, and the steering committee provides access to resources.[3]

---

3. Rosabeth Moss Kanter has developed this perspective in far greater detail than is appropriate here. See Kanter (1983, Chapter 7).

The Morphogenic Metaphor

This view comes from a systems theory of the evolution of human systems.[4] The theory is that human systems naturally adapt and evolve when individual roles contain enough ambiguity. Each time a new person occupies an existing role, he or she slightly changes the role to fit his or her proclivities and the requirements he or she faces. Over time, through the succession of different individuals occupying a role, the role naturally evolves and adapts to contextual demands. As different roles each go through this process of adaptation, the system as a whole evolves. This is the morphogenic process of human systems.

If there is not enough ambiguity in the role, however, this morphogenic process gets blocked and the system stagnates. In tightly designed bureaucracies with highly prescribed roles, the process of organizational adaptation may get stifled by highly constrained role definitions (such as strictly defined responsibilities, highly routinized tasks, and very compartmentalized jobs). In such systems, a parallel learning structure opens up the opportunity for people to create new roles and recreate old ones. Things that haven't been questioned in the past can now be questioned. People can take on new tasks and responsibilities. Therefore, the reason the parallel learning structure causes change is that the morphogenic process has been unleashed.

The Political Metaphor

From this point of view, politics is the process of organizational governance and involves the negotiation and bargaining of means and ends.[5] Organizations vary in the degree to which they provide members with access to forums where the ends (e.g., goals, purposes, missions, objectives) and means (e.g., strategies, tactics, procedures, work processes) of the organization are negotiated and agreed upon. These forums can include anything from official meetings to informal conversations on the golf course.

---

4. Buckley (1967).

5. Tichy (1983).

Machine bureaucracies like the military and factories tend to have a fairly high degree of consensus on means and ends by virtue of the fact that a very limited number of people have access to forums where means and ends are negotiated. In these cases, the parallel structure causes change by creating a new forum for bargaining and negotiation that includes many people who, in the past, had been disenfranchised. This has two key effects. First, it disrupts the status quo and generates a period of time when there is, at the very least, a lack of consensus on some of the means. Second, it increases the diversity of perspectives that must be accommodated to attain a new consensus.

Professional bureaucracies like hospitals and universities, on the other hand, tend to have a fairly low degree of consensus on organizational means and ends and a number of competing factions with roughly equal power. Such bureaucracies can become paralyzed by an inability to create a coalition strong enough to direct the organization. Here the parallel learning structure can create change by providing a time and space for members of these opposing factions to learn to appreciate each other's perspectives and develop shared understandings.[6]

The Cell-Mutation Metaphor

Cell replication is the process by which living organisms recreate exact copies of themselves. A code (DNA) organizes the patterning of materials and processes so that each new cell is identical in function and operation to the last. Cells may deviate (mutate) if there are sufficient changes in their electrochemical environment. Without gross intrusions, however, cells continue to replicate reliably.

From this perspective, the parallel learning structure creates change by causing mutations in "cell replication." When simple task forces or committees are set up, they almost invariably replicate the organization's "code" (assumptions, operating procedures, norms, patterns of interaction). Yet, it is exactly the limitations of these patterns that has created the need for the intervention. Here, useful mutations in the organization's code are needed to aid in adapting

---

6. For more on this, see Bushe and Shani (1990).

to a changed environment. By creating a visibly distinct structure to house interaction, the environment at work is changed and the process of mutation is encouraged and enhanced.

The Morphic Resonance Metaphor

This perspective comes from a new and controversial theory of the repetition of biological, physical, and even social forms.[7] Events that, from an energetic point of view, should not be predictable from the outset are actually limited in the forms they can assume by "morphogenetic fields." Once a form exists, it sends off a morphic resonance, like a radio signal, that exists across space and time. New situations that have the right combination of factors can then pick up this morphic resonance and recreate that form. The probability that other similar situations will create a similar form is increased the more that form has existed in the past.

When applied to parallel learning structures, the morphic resonance metaphor highlights the possibilities for change in the forms of interaction within the total organization by changing the forms of interaction within the parallel learning structure. For many years, OD consultants and researchers have traded anecdotes about changes in a microcosm (like a small group) seeming to have inexplicably caused changes in a macrocosm (like an organization). The most common observation is how a consulting team may develop the same dysfunctional form of interaction as the client system. This is usually seen as an opportunity for diagnosing client-system dynamics by diagnosing consulting-team behavior. Sometimes, after the consulting team has worked on itself, the client system appears also to magically change. Similarly, we have observed changes in relations between people from different constituencies in a parallel structure group presage similar changes between the constituencies in the organization at large that cannot be explained by conventional notions of cause and effect.

The Chaos Metaphor

From this point of view, nonlinear systems (and as far as we know, all human systems are nonlinear) maintain stability among inter-

---

7. Sheldrake (1981).

connected parts until a key variable is pushed over a threshold. Then, a system's point of equilibrium shifts radically to another point that cannot be predicted in advance. The system either reconstitutes itself at a higher level of complexity or it disintegrates and becomes nonrecognizable.[8]

Parallel learning structures create change because they multiply interconnections and push a key variable (the change focus) and in doing so force a re-examination of the organization's processes. A key variable that many organizations are trying to push these days is "quality." In health care, the new variable being driven is "cost." As a variable is driven (not simply talked about), everything else in the system begins to "creak." Old values and accepted practices and patterns of organizing become threatened. If the variable is really pushed, the organization comes to a threshold and may well back off, fearing the mounting anxiety that chaos creates. If the organization pushes through that threshold, it is often on the basis of faith, because there are few if any role models for what kind of organization it will become. If the organization cannot reorganize that chaos into a new, though more complex, stable pattern, it probably won't survive. If, on the other hand, the organization is able to redesign itself around the driving variable, it will probably be in a much more developed and competitive form.

Applying the Metaphors to the Cases

A review of the cases in this book from the perspective of these metaphors reveals different understandings of the change processes in each case. At Grate Hospital, the most applicable description of the change process observed is the political metaphor. The parallel structure led to a break with the status quo and the beginning of a process of developing a shared understanding of an important means of achieving the hospital's goal of quality patient care. People who had not been able to contribute to the discussions about how to achieve this goal now had an avenue for input. In effect, the parallel structure opened up a new forum for negotiating the "means" of quality care. Though not highlighted in the case, the morphic

---

8. For more information on the science of chaos, written for the lay reader, see Prigogine and Stengers (1984) and Gleick (1987).

resonance metaphor may explain a noticeable reduction in tension between doctors and others in the hospital after the confrontation in the study group.

At Intercon Semiconductor, the rational brain and intrapreneurial metaphors describe a good portion of the process of change observed. Problems were clarified and groups worked at devising solutions to those, which were then implemented. The parallel learning structure created the network opportunities to share and access corporate-wide resources. Having the collective organizational knowledge within each of the groups sparked the energy for inquiry and learning about how the corporation "really operated." The empowerment of the parallel structure to develop specific proposals unleashed individual creativity during the ongoing change process.

The rational-brain, political, intrapreneurial, morphic resonance, and chaos metaphors each describe salient change processes at Triburg Manufacturing. (Not all of this is clear from the brief case description.) While many of these streams of change took place outside the formal parallel structure, their interweaving was critical to the total project. Individuals who identified ways of applying SPC were encouraged to take personal initiative in doing so (intrapreneurial metaphor). The whole effort raised a host of questions about how to best run a manufacturing facility, raising doubts especially about the wisdom of having separate service functions and the traditional emphasis on labor efficiency in assessing an area's performance (political metaphor). There was a noticeable increase in cooperation between service and manufacturing managers at all levels of the hierarchy after the "revolt" by service and manufacturing department heads (morphic resonance). Finally, multiplying interconnections and driving quality as a key variable (chaos metaphor) pushed the organization into much greater complexity on many fronts: its understanding of its own manufacturing processes, how it assessed performance, its management of interdepartmental interdependencies, its relationships with suppliers and divisional staffs, to name but a few. While the organization had not reached a threshold in the time span reported in this case, it did a few years after.

At Pittown Assembly, there was not much "rationality" in the change process. Most of the improvements in performance and climate did not come from groups devising "solutions." The failure of the first union-management committee can be understood from the cell-mutation metaphor. The committee simply did what joint committees had always done in the past—collective bargaining. A mutation in senior management-union relations was needed and occurred through the unprecedented act of the top three officers of the plant and the union going on a trip together. The political and morphogenic metaphors provide good explanations of the change process that followed. Politically, those who had had little access to forums of decision making (i.e., the union, workers, lower-level managers) now had a great deal more. Just as important, however, was the tremendous evolution in roles that occurred during the project. The managers' and supervisors' style shifted from authoritarian to participative. Worker roles changed to become more involved in decisions affecting their work processes. Union reps dropped their hostile, adversarial roles and became representatives of the common good. What the parallel structure did was provide an opportunity to loosen up the rigid pattern of roles that had been in place for many years.

In the Military Data Processing Unit we saw the strongest case of the problems of cell replication. It took almost half a year for the study group to start mutating out of patterns of interaction one expects to find in the military. In this case, the force for mutation was clearly the external consultants. At each meeting, they had to reinforce the sense that "now we're taking our shirts off," symbolizing that different hierarchical levels (denoted by emblems on one's shirt) did not exist in the room. There also seemed to be some morphic resonance activated by the confrontation between military and civilian personnel in the study group. After this, relations between these groups on the base noticeably improved. After these changes, the rational-brain metaphor seems to best capture the process of redesign undertaken by the DPU and the changes that took place.

Using Metaphors of Change

From the change agent's point of view, it is important to identify which metaphors of change he or she is explicitly and implicitly using to guide the day-to-day interpretation of events and decisions that must get made. The same events can take on an optimistic or pessimistic tone, depending on what you're looking for and what your hopes are. Take, for example, the following scenario: Six months after the parallel structure is up and running, a senior manager who has had little to do with the project comes into your office and begins ranting and raving about the mess this whole thing is creating. The manager says that the projects the groups are working on are irrelevant and that the intervention is causing problems with the orderly execution of tasks. From the rational-brain perspective, this sounds like bad news. Your first inclination would probably be to get the groups back "on track" and ensure that they are doing "productive work." From the political perspective, this could be good or bad news, depending on the degree to which you are trying to open up the system and empower subordinates. From a cell-mutation point of view, you'd want to know before doing anything if the "mutations" this manager is ranting about are dangerous or adaptive. From the morphogenic or chaos points of view, however, this is definitely good news, and you know the intervention is working.

Try another scenario: A year after the parallel learning structure is created, a few thorny problems have been identified and solved. Groups have an air of "business as usual," and though not many employees are that interested in being involved, the ones that are are motivated and productive. From the rational-brain metaphor, it looks like the parallel structure is working fine. From the intrapreneurial metaphor, you might be a little concerned that more people aren't signing up, but otherwise things are going well. From the cell-mutation metaphor, you'd assess whether enough mutation had occurred for the time being and act accordingly. From the morphogenic, political, and/or chaos perspectives, however, it looks like the intervention has had little effect and drastic action is required to salvage it.

Whom should one include in the initial set-up of a parallel structure? The answers to this vary by the metaphor of change you use. For example, should people with a history of mutual antagonism be put into the same group? If a reduction of antagonism in the organization is what you seek, then the morphic resonance metaphor strongly suggests this course. From the rational-brain and intrapreneurial metaphors, however, this looks like a dumb move.

In promoting and guiding a change process, it is very important to be aware of the metaphor(s) you are operating out of, and if they are very different from other key players in your system, you probably need to do some informal educating and coaching about what constitutes progress and what should be considered a problem as the change process unfolds. In most cases, you will probably be operating out of a combination of these (and maybe other) metaphors. No one metaphor is correct. It is probably most effective to be able to use all of them in planning for and maintaining a viable change effort.

9

Conclusion

In this book we have tried to convey the potential merits of parallel learning structures without (hopefully) falling into the traps of overenthusiasm or naive idealism. We have tried to highlight that it is not so much the structure, but the processes that get housed in that structure, that determine the success or failure of the parallel learning structure. And we have tried to emphasize the importance of theory for the manager and consultant using a parallel structure. Without a theoretical understanding of the change processes one is trying to accomplish, techniques themselves are of little value.

We have identified and discussed five purposes for which parallel learning structures can be used. No doubt, others will find more. It seems to be a useful intervention whenever we want people to change their way of interacting to generate more learning, while still producing the outputs the organization expects from them. While some people are able to change their styles of thinking and relating readily, most of us can't. We need social and psychological supports to act differently in the same situation. When implemented effectively, the parallel learning structure provides the support for a way of interacting and solving problems that bureaucratic efficiencies just can't tolerate. Through the symbolic context of the parallel learning structure, people seem to be able to shift modes of thinking and relating from performance-oriented in the formal structure, to learning-oriented in the parallel structure, and back again.

Implementing a parallel learning structure is not a decision to be taken lightly. It is an expensive remedy. It takes time and money to train internal facilitators and to allow people to meet in groups to work on issues. It may not produce visible results for a long time, and it's not that easy to control once it's up and running. In addition, premature termination of a parallel structure that has captured employees' excitement and energy by senior managers who are threatened by loss of control may cause more harm to the system and people in it than never having tried it in the first place.

Yet, for some problems, like implementing system-transforming innovations or developing cooperative labor relations, it almost seems indispensable. And it has important possibilities for designing organizations for simultaneous efficiency and innovation and for sociotechnical redesigns. Over the past ten years as we have worked with this intervention, we have been struck by how many consultants, managers, and organizations instinctively set up parallel structures to promote large system changes without even considering the technostructural implications of that action, let alone the need to develop a different culture within the structure. There is an intuitive rightness about the intervention for certain kinds of change processes. But parallel structures are rarely recognized as a new organizing form, and as such there has been little research on them and not much guidance for practitioners in their use. We hope this book helps managers and consultants to see and more clearly understand the parallel structures they are currently using and helps them be more thoughtful and effective in their use. Our hope is that the book stimulates further research on structures and processes that engender innovation, productivity, cooperation, adaptation, and learning in bureaucratic organizations.

Appendix A

Sociotechnical Systems Theory: A Brief Synopsis

The sociotechnical systems (STS) school of thought provides a theoretical and practical framework for understanding, designing, transforming, and managing work organizations. Since its development in the early 1950s, interest in its use has grown steadily and the theory and methods of STS have evolved considerably. STS theory considers every organization a sociotechnical system, though not every organization is designed with that in mind. Published reports of STS applications in a variety of organizations around the globe indicate that organizations designed this way have more success in improving productivity, effectiveness, and quality of work life than traditional work designs.[1]

The backbone of STS theory is the principle of joint optimization, which states that organizations should be designed to jointly optimize the demands of the technical and the social systems to fit with the organization's environment. In STS, the relationship between business strategy, technology, productivity, and human resources is emphasized. STS is a flexible design theory that encourages organizational choice instead of insisting that there is one best way to organize work.

Different theorists have identified different STS design principles, and we reviewed some of these in Chapter 6. The most recent (Pasmore, 1988) has grouped these into six key categories: (1)

---

1. Pasmore, Francis, Haldeman, and Shani (1982).

encouraging innovation versus preserving the status quo; (2) developing human resources; (3) developing awareness of the external environment; (4) maximizing cooperative effort; (5) developing commitment and energy; and (6) utilizing social and technical resources effectively.

STS design and redesign processes are elaborate, multilevel organization development efforts. They follow the action-research method and involve business-environment analysis, vision and strategy formulation, system analysis and diagnosis, exploration of alternatives for joint optimization, experimental implementation, and system-wide diffusion. Usually some form of parallel learning structure is created to carry out the effort. Mutual education and learning between consultants and organizational members is an integral part of the STS redesign project. Typically, just as in the semiconductor and military cases reported in this book, a seminar or set of seminars on the design and management of sociotechnical systems would set the stage for the entire project. The seminars are usually an intensive experience that can run anywhere from three to ten days. Cases reported in this book had seminars that covered theoretical foundations of STS, high-performing work systems and cultures, an in-depth examination of STS design principles, and a review of alternative STS change models, phases, processes, and support structures. They included visits to sites that had implemented an STS redesign and provided an exploration of specific STS analytic methods and techniques (such as variance analysis of the linear and nonlinear systems, variance matrix, and open-systems planning).

Good introductory sources on STS design principles are Emery and Trist (1973), Cherns (1978), Kolodny and Dresner (1986), Hanna (1988), Schultheiss (1988), and Shani and Elliott (1990), as well as the special issue on STS in the *Journal of Applied Behavioral Science* (22:3, 1986). The most complete recent statement on STS design is Pasmore (1988).

Appendix B

Developing a Parallel Learning Structure: A Simulation

Explaining to managers what a parallel learning structure is and how it works can be a challenge. It isn't often that you can take a top-management team (or the steering committee or the parallel learning structure) to see an organization that has implemented one for the same reasons as your organization. To fill this void, we have developed a simulation that can be used in a classroom setting and in a basic training session.[1]

The simulation has three broadly defined goals:

1. To allow participants to recognize bureaucratic barriers to problem solving within an organization.
2. To demonstrate the use of parallel learning structure interventions toward more optimal utilization of human resources.
3. To develop methods for cross-boundary organizational dialogue mechanisms within bureaucratic structures

Group Size

From 18 to 35 participants.

---

1. A first draft of this simulation was developed in collaboration with Daniel Wise.

Time Required

Two to four hours. Minimum times for each activity are shown in brackets.

Materials

1. A copy of the Prairie General Hospital case description for each participant.
2. One role description for each participant.
3. A newsprint flip chart and felt-tipped marker for each group (optimally 3).
4. Masking tape for posting the newsprint.
5. Name tags and marker pens.

Physical Setting

A room large enough so that groups may work without disturbing one another. Movable chairs should be available.

Process

1. The facilitator explains that participants will be exploring the functioning of a bureaucratic organization by playing roles within that organization. The facilitator then describes the organization, paying particular attention to descriptions of the various departments and identifying the management hierarchy of the organization. (5 minutes)
2. Participants divide into nine role-playing groups with three-to-six members in each. Each group represents one of the professional groups present on the organization chart (i.e., MDs, residents, interns, registered nurses, nursing assistants, physical/occupational therapists, social services, and maintenance engineers. The ninth group is made up of the CEO, medical director, and administrative director.) Each participant should have a copy of the Prairie General Hospital (PGH) case description and the appropriate role description. They read these. Each group member prepares a name tag, which iden-

tifies his or her professional group. Participants then spend time in these groups developing their assumed personalities. The following issues are helpful in developing a group identity:

Who are we?

What is our professional identity?

What are our likes and dislikes at PGH?

All groups except registered nurses and social services should select a leader and spokesperson. The head nurse and social services director will lead these groups. (20 minutes)

3. The groups generate a list of potential issues facing them, their departments, and the organization. At least three issues should be identified. (10 minutes)

4. Three problem-solving groups are formed, each having one director or the CEO and one member from each of the professional groups. Additional participants, if any, observe the groups' functioning. The groups discuss the issues identified by the departments and then choose three high-priority issues to be addressed by management. These problems are written on the flip charts and posted. (10 minutes)

5. STOP. The class is reassembled, and the facilitator leads participants in a discussion of the major characteristics of the current organization. Specific issues for this discussion might include the following:

What is the level of shared understanding achieved within the various groups?

How could that shared understanding be enhanced?

Are group members communicating with each other?

How effective is communication across professional group boundaries?

What are the current challenges faced by the organization?

What are the strengths and weaknesses of the organization?

What area(s) need improvement? (15 minutes)

6. The facilitator describes the concept of parallel learning structures along the following lines: Parallel learning structures operate outside the bureaucratic structure of an organization. Members of the parallel learning structure are also members of the larger organization. A parallel structure is made up of a steering committee and one or more study/action groups. The steering committee selects problems for the parallel structure to examine and provides direction for that effort. The steering committee acts as an interface between the parallel structure and upper-level management. Action/study groups are composed of members from all levels of the organization. Guidelines for action/study group meetings include a disregard for bureaucratic rank and the encouragement of communications across professional group boundaries. All participants in the action group are given equal voice in discussions. Decisions are made by consensus. Leadership rotates among group members. The aim of the action/study groups is to reach mutual understanding and to benefit from the contributions of each member.

Once the characteristics of the parallel learning structure are understood, review Steps 7–12 before continuing. (10 minutes)

7. A steering committee is formed consisting of the CEO, the two directors, the head nurse, and the chosen representative from the medical doctors' group. The steering committee meets in a "fishbowl," with members of each professional group observing from outside the perimeter. The steering committee chooses three issues affecting the organization. These may be different from those identified in Step 4. Again, the issues identified should be written on flip charts. (7 minutes)

8. Participants reconvene in their professional units. Their new tasks are to: (1) get one or two volunteers to serve on each of the three groups dealing with the three issues identified in Step 7; and (2) refine the group's point of view on each of those issues. (15 minutes)

9. Three action groups assemble, one for each problem identified in Step 7. The groups should assemble around a flip chart identifying the problem they will be working with.

Each group is composed of the volunteers from Step 8 plus one of the three upper managers. It is best if the members of the steering committee are spread evenly among the three groups. Remaining class members can assemble around the groups and observe the process. Action/study group members symbolically remove name tags and thus relinquish their hierarchical position within the action group. Each group selects a leader. The action/study groups clearly define the problem they are considering. They then seek alternative solutions, define criteria for choosing a solution, and develop a proposed solution for steering committee review. (30 minutes)

The important shift to look for, and the key lesson of this simulation, is that in this second round the study group members develop an organization-wide appreciation of the problems, unlike the first time they met (Step 4) where each person primarily focused on the point of view of his or her respective department.

10. The steering committee meets again, with nonmembers observing. The committee reviews the proposals and develops an implementation strategy and a strategy for presentation to the formal organizational leadership. (10 minutes)

11. STOP. The reassembled class identifies the characteristics of the parallel structure. Positive characteristics may include an organization-wide appreciation of the issues, collaboration across department boundaries, changed communication flow, improved problem-solving capability, and greater trust among group members. Shortcomings may include apprehension regarding changed status, confusion about roles, and distrust of the process and the motives of management. (10 minutes)

12. The facilitator leads a concluding discussion comparing the operation of the "new" organization with that of the old. Appropriate discussion questions include:

What are the advantages of each type of organization?

What are the disadvantages?

To what extent does structural change influence outcomes?

What differences in communication effectiveness, organizational culture, and problem-solving effectiveness were apparent?

What are the effects of structure on output?

What are the effects on quality of working relationships? How do these differences affect output? (10 minutes)

Variations

1. Larger and smaller classes can be accommodated by increasing or decreasing the number of problems generated and action groups that address them.

2. Total time for the simulation can be reduced by running the parallel structure and the traditional structure at the same time. Observers can take notes and then compare the operation of both groups.

3. Step 11 can be eliminated in the interest of time. In this case, it is important to note that the steering committee would normally present the solutions to the organizational hierarchy during the discussion in Step 12.

Case Description: Prairie General Hospital

Prairie General Hospital is a research hospital associated with a large university in the Midwest. PGH has an 85-year history and a reputation for excellence and innovation. That reputation has been built upon a genuine concern for the public welfare, as well as the quality of the medical school program.

Recently, the university's board of regents decided that PGH should stand on its own feet financially. Up until now, it has relied on university funds for its continued existence. As a result of this new attitude, several policies have been changed, most notably the way uninsured patients are treated. For the most part, these patients are referred to the county hospital across town. Other policies have changed, too, including a reduction of support staff, closing of the gift shop, and cutbacks in the acquisition of state-of-the-art equipment.

PGH is organized in two major clusters—medical and administration (see Fig. B.1). The chief executive officer of Prairie

Figure B.1
Prairie General Hospital: Organization Chart

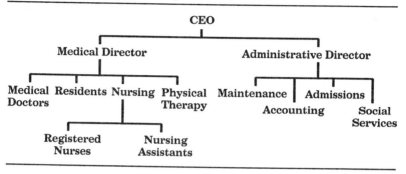

General Hospital, together with the medical director and the administrative director, are charged with the responsibility of managing the hospital. Each of the two major subsystems, with their own mix of personnel, tasks, and technologies, is composed of multiple professional departments.

The local newspapers have been devoting a great deal of attention to what's been happening at PGH recently. According to their reports, the board of directors recently rejected a new nuclear magnetic resonance imaging lab and has trimmed the medical staff. The public is beginning to wonder about the reliability of Prairie General.

Hospital CEO (1)

PGH is a university-associated hospital, so the role of CEO, which you recently accepted, is a misnomer. You report to a board of directors, as well as the university president. You also have the board of regents over your head. The university has seen the trend toward higher profits in the hospital industry, and they want PGH to fall in line and reduce the demands made on the university's already stretched budget. You have spent most of your career in hospital administration. You were hired to run PGH four months ago. This is your first time in a research hospital.

The mood at PGH has been down lately, due to increased pressure by the board to increase profits, staff changes, and increased demands by the union executive. You have been working diligently to reconcile conflicts. However, your success has been limited. Meetings with the hospital administrators have been nightmarish. Tempers have been short, yelling frequent, and accusations all too freely dispensed. In your opinion, very little is accomplished at these meetings, and the hospital would be better off if you, the medical director, and the administrative services director made all the decisions. To hell with the rest of them!

You are scheduled to chair another meeting this afternoon. On the agenda are complaints about staffing shortages, admissions-policy recommendations, and a restructuring proposition. There is also a free spot in the agenda for department heads to voice their complaints and make open recommendations for action. You dread this monthly ritual.

Hospital Administrative Director (1)

As hospital administrative director, you are responsible for the day-to-day operations of PGH. You oversee all nonmedical functions, including admissions, billing, staff assignments, and making sure the lights and elevators work. Personnel who report directly to you include the social services director, the admissions director, the head maintenance engineer, the nursing director, and the accounting department director. You also have people to take care of billing and supplies. Your training is in health care administration. You have an MBA and an MA in public health administration. You have been in this position for ten years and at PGH for eighteen years. You work hard, believe that hospitals should be profitable, and admire those members of your staff who are willing to put in a little extra time to get things done. The increasing difficulty of collecting Medicare money has been a recent nemesis. As a result, you are very vocal about establishing policies to limit the admission of indigent patients. You are at odds with the medical director on this point.

Medical Director (1)

You have been at PGH for ten years. You are now in charge of the medical aspects of hospital administration, an office you have held for a little over six months. You are trained as an MD, and sometimes you wish you could spend time on the floor treating patients. As it is, you spend a lot of time in your office doing paper work or making telephone calls. Most of your time, though, seems to be taken up in endless meetings with various division chiefs or with the hospital board of directors. Recent trends have driven PGH to tighter business practices, affecting admissions and treatment policies. You can understand the need for making the hospital work like a well-run business, but you still wish your staff could treat patients as people a little more often.

You used to get along well with most of the hospital staff. However, you now find that the doctors, nurses, and even the orderlies and staff seem to avoid you and rarely talk to you. You've found yourself sitting alone in the cafeteria more often than you appreciate. You take your administrative role seriously, and you like to get things done at meetings. You follow a tight agenda and make many decisions on your own.

Medical Doctors (3–6)

You have a private practice outside of the hospital and alternate days at each. You are on call several days a week. You live 30 minutes from the hospital. You receive a good income but work long hours. You spend little extra time at the hospital; your time there is spent with patients. You appreciate the work of the nursing staff, but you have little time to spare to talk with them. You feel pressured by the hospital administration to cut corners in treating patients. The administration has recently stressed the importance of cutting costs. You feel the new admissions guidelines prevent you from giving appropriate care to your patients. You consider yourself more knowledgeable and therefore in a superior position to make decisions about patient care and hospital policy. You resent the seemingly endless committee meetings that have recently occupied your time.

Residents (3–6)

You completed medical school a year ago—eight years of school and a year of internship living on borrowed money and a shoe string. Now you are receiving $1,600 a month, and you are expected to work twenty-four-hour shifts four or more days per week. You are tired. Your family "never" sees you, and your children are growing up. You have all the responsibility for patient care, but you receive none of the credit. In other words, you feel you are being used as cheap labor.

You are not represented by a union. You are represented at hospital administrative meetings by your department's chief physician. You do interact with the doctors and nurses on your floor, but you feel several of the physicians consider you inferior and do not trust your judgment.

Head Nurse (1)

You have been with the hospital for eight years, most of that time in the intensive care unit. You were recently transferred to obstetrics and appointed head nurse there. You are frustrated that you have not had the time to get to know the nurses who are working with you in the new department, and you have sensed discontent within the department. You are aware that there has been a chronic shortage of nursing staff, and that the nurses have been asked to work extra shifts, sometimes back-to-back with their scheduled shifts. You are also frustrated that the doctors seem to ignore the nurses, yet the nurses do most of the work in preparing mothers for delivery. You represent the nurses in your department at regular hospital administrative meetings. Recently, the nurses gave you a list of grievances. The list included:

work-scheduling problems (extra shifts)

low pay

hold-up of instruments in sterilization facility

understaffing

the medical director's attitude

Registered Nurses (3–6)

You are a registered nurse in the obstetrics section. You normally work twelve-hour shifts four days a week. You are often called to work an extra shift, sometimes back-to-back, due to scheduling problems and chronic shortages of personnel. You consider yourself underpaid and overworked, especially considering your level of training and the hours you are called upon to serve. You feel relatively powerless in the hierarchy, and you are represented by the nurses' union. Recently, a nurse from another department was appointed head nurse. Several nurses within the department feel they should have been given the position. The new head nurse is demanding and difficult to get along with.

Nursing Assistants (3–6)

Yours is an hourly position, the average rate being six dollars per hour. You perform menial jobs on the floor: changing linens, transporting patients within the hospital, preparing surgical equipment, and assisting the nurses. You are not represented by the union. Your hours are flexible and change from week to week. You have not been able to schedule events in your personal life because of the unpredictability of the schedule. Your major contact at the hospital is with the nurses. The head nurse represents your interests at the administrative meetings.

Physical/Occupational Therapists (3–6)

As a physical or occupational therapist, you report to the medical director. You work with patients who have undergone surgery or suffered a debilitating illness, such as a stroke. Most of your work is on a one-on-one basis with the patients. You enjoy your work and especially like to note the progress of your patients. This kind of therapy is usually long-term, and many of your patients are outpatients. You try not to get involved in the political/monetary issues of PGH, but you have not been able to avoid noticing that your patients have been more tense and have been scheduling less time with you. You suspect it is due to the billing practices and policies of the hospital administration. The head of your department recently retired and has not been replaced. As a result, your department is not currently represented at hospital administrative meetings.

Social Services Director (1)

The social services department provides inpatient and outpatient services to PGH's customers. These services include financial counseling, public seminars, drug-therapy programs, and family-support groups. You consider the services of your department critical to the public image of the hospital. Your staff consists of nonmedical professionals, including social workers, psychologists, and marketing professionals. These individuals are highly competent and like to work on their own with little supervision. You get along well with your staff, respecting their individuality and always able to compliment their work. Lately, however, the administrative director has been attempting to cut the budget of your department. He or she feels that the hospital could save money by cutting back the "superfluous" services offered by your department. You vehemently disagree.

Social Services Staff (3–6)

The social services department runs many of the outpatient programs for PGH, such as drug and alcohol rehabilitation, family-support groups, public-health seminars, and financial counseling. You also handle the publicity for those programs. The staff consists of nonmedical professionals, including social workers, psychologists, and marketing experts. You can choose to be any one of these. You consider yourself highly competent and resent unnecessary supervision when working with your clients.

The social services department is clustered with the administrative functions of PGH. Your immediate supervisor is the social services director, who reports to the hospital administrative director. You get along well with your supervisor. You have very little contact with the administrative director. You feel that the services provided by your department could be better represented by the medical director. Recent cutbacks in "superfluous services" convince you of that fact. There are rumors about that staff cuts are imminent.

Maintenance Engineers (Maintenance) (2)

If it weren't for the two of you, PGH would have shut down fifteen years ago. You are the people who keep the heat running when it's 10° below outside and the air conditioning on when it's 95°. If there is a problem with the electrical circuits, or the oxygen, or anything else in the hospital, you and your staff will get it working again. But usually there are not any problems, because you keep on top of things. Then again, there isn't any credit given, since everything seems to work so well.

Your crew is on duty twenty-four hours a day. They're a good bunch and know what they are doing. Nonetheless, you are on call at all times in case of an emergency they can't handle. For some reason, you have been called in far too often in the last several months. Something is going wrong. You've talked to your crew about it, but they have not been able to help you figure out why things are breaking. It all seemed to start when that new CEO came to roost as chief honcho. Well, you do your job, and so does the rest of the engineering staff. Besides, you'll be retiring soon, so it doesn't much matter what people at PGH are up to.

Bibliography

Acar, W., Melcher, A. J., and Aupperle, K. E. 1987. The implementation of innovation strategies. Paper presented at the Annual Meeting of the Academy of Management, New Orleans, August.

Ackoff, R. L. 1981. *Creating the Corporate Future.* New York: Wiley.

Adizes, I. 1979. Organizational Passages: Diagnosing and treating lifecycle problems of organizations. *Organizational Dynamics* (Summer): 3–25.

Alderfer, C. P. 1987. An intergroup perspective on group dynamics. In *Handbook of Organizational Behavior,* ed. J. Lorsch, pp. 190–222. Englewood Cliffs, NJ: Prentice-Hall.

Bart, C. 1988. Organizing for the new product development. *Journal of Business Strategy* 9:34–38.

Beckhard, R. 1969. *Organization Development: Strategies and Models.* Reading, MA: Addison-Wesley.

Bennis, W. G. 1966. *Beyond Bureaucracy.* New York: McGraw-Hill.

Brekelmans, W., and Jonsson, B. 1976. The diffusion of work design changes in Volvo. *Columbia Journal of World Business* (Summer): 96–99.

Buckley, W. 1967. *Sociology and Modern Systems Theory.* Englewood Cliffs, NJ: Prentice-Hall.

Bushe, G. R. 1988a. Developing cooperative labor-management relations in unionized factories: A multi-case study of quality circles and parallel organization within joint QWL projects. *Journal of Applied Behavioral Science* 24:129–50.

———. 1988b. Cultural contradictions of statistical process control in American manufacturing organizations. *Journal of Management* 14:19–31.

————. 1985. *Dynamics of Implementing Statistical Process Control: A Behavioral Science Perspective*. Ottawa, Ontario: Department of Regional Industrial Expansion, Government of Canada.

Bushe, G. R., Danko, D., and Long, K. J. 1984. A structure for successful worker problem-solving groups. In *Matrix Management Systems Handbook*, ed. D. Cleland, pp. 714–31. New York: Von Nostrand Reinhold, 714–31.

Bushe, G. R., and Shani, A. B. 1990. Parallel learning structure interventions in bureaucratic organizations. In *Research in Organizational Change and Development, Volume 4*, eds. R. W. Woodman and W. A. Pasmore, pp. 193–220. Greenwich, CT: JAI Press.

Cherns, A. 1978. The principles of sociotechnical design. In *Sociotechnical Systems*, eds. W. A. Pasmore and J. J. Sherwood, pp. 61–71. La Jolla, CA: University Associates.

Cohn, S. F., and Turyn, R. M. 1984. Organizational structure, decision-making procedures, and the adoption of innovations. *IEEE Transactions on Engineering Management* 31:154–61.

Collier, J. 1946. United States Indian administration as a laboratory of ethnic relations. *Social Research* 12:275–86.

Crosby, P. B. 1979. *Quality Is Free*. New York: McGraw-Hill.

Cummings, T. G. 1986. Future directions of sociotechnical systems theory and research. *Journal of Applied Behavioral Science* 22:355–60.

Daft, R. L. 1978. A dual-core model of organizational innovation. *Academy of Management Journal* 21:193–210.

Dahrendorf, R. 1959. *Class and Class Conflict in Industrial Society*. Stanford, CA: Stanford University.

Downs, G. W., and Mohr, L. B. 1976. Conceptual issues in the study of innovation. *Administrative Science Quarterly* 21:700–14.

Drexler, J. A., and Lawler, E. E. 1977. A union-management cooperative project to improve the quality of work life. *Journal of Applied Behavioral Science* 13:373–87.

Duncan, R. B. 1976. The ambidextrous organization: Designing dual structures for innovation. In *The Management of Organizational Design: Volume 1*, eds. R. H. Kilmann, L. R. Pondy, and D. P. Slevin, pp. 167–88. New York: Elsevier North-Holland.

Eden, D. 1988. Creating expectation effects in OD: Applying self-fulfilling prophecy. In *Research in Organizational Change and Development*,

Volume 2, eds. R. W. Woodman and W. A. Pasmore, pp. 235–67. Greenwich, CT: JAI Press.

Emery, F. E., and Thorsrud, E. 1976. *Democracy at Work.* Leiden, Neth.: Martinus Nijhoff.

Emery, F. E., and Trist, E. 1973. *Towards a Social Ecology.* New York: Plenum.

Ettlie, J. E., Bridges, W. P., and O'Keefe, R.D. 1984. Organization strategy and structural differences for radical versus incremental innovation. *Management Science* 30:682–95.

Friedlander, F., and Brown, L. D. 1974. Organization Development. *Annual Review of Psychology* 25:313–41.

Galbraith, J. R. 1982. The innovating organization. *Organizational Dynamics* (Winter): 5–25.

———. 1977. *Organization Design.* Reading, MA: Addison-Wesley.

Gamson, W. A. 1968. *Power and Discontent.* Homewood, IL: Dorsey.

Garvin, D. A. 1983. Quality on the line. *Harvard Business Review* (Sept.–Oct.): 64–75.

Georgopoulos, B. S. 1981. Distinguishing organizational features of hospitals. In *Improving Health Care Management,* ed. G. F. Wieland. Ann Arbor, MI: Health Administration Press.

Gleick, J. 1987. *Chaos.* New York: Penguin.

Goldratt, E. M., and Cox, J. 1986. *The Goal: A Process of Ongoing Improvement.* Croton-on-Hudson, NY: North River Press.

Goldsmith, J. C. 1980. The health care market: Can hospitals survive? *Harvard Business Review* (July–Aug.): 100–12.

Goldstein, S. G. 1985. Organizational dualism and quality circles. *Academy of Management Review* 10:504–17.

———. 1978. A structure for change. *Human Relations* 31:957–83.

Greenbaum, H. H., Holden, E. J., and Spataro, L. 1983. Organizational structure and communication processes: A study of change. *Group and Organization Studies* 8:61–82.

Hackman, J. R., and Oldham, G. 1980. *Work Redesign.* Reading, MA: Addison-Wesley.

Hanna, P. 1988. *Designing Organizations for High Performance.* Reading, MA: Addison-Wesley.

Hawley, J. A. 1984. Transforming organizations through vertical linking. *Organizational Dynamics* (Winter): 68–80.

Herrick, N. Q. 1985. Parallel organizations in unionized settings: Implications for organizational research. *Human Relations* 38:963–81.

Jaques, E. 1989. *Requisite Organization.* Arlington, VA: Cason Hall.

Kanter, R. M. 1983. *The Change Masters.* New York: Basic Books.

Kilmann, R. H. 1989. *Managing Beyond the Quick Fix.* San Francisco: Jossey-Bass.

————. 1982. Designing collateral organizations. *Human Systems Management* 3:66–76.

Kolb, D. A. 1984. *Experiential Learning.* Englewood Cliffs, NJ: Prentice-Hall.

Kolodny, H., and Dresner, B. 1986. Linking arrangements and new work designs. *Organizational Dynamics* (Winter): 33–51.

Lawrence, P. R., and Dyer, D. 1983. *Renewing American Industry.* New York: Free Press.

Levitt, B., and March, J. G. 1988. Organizational learning. *Annual Review of Sociology* 14:319–40.

Lewin, K. 1946. Action research and minority problems. *Journal of Social Issues* 2:34–36.

MacKenzie, K. 1986. *Organization Design.* New York: Ablex.

Margulies, N., and Adams, J., eds. 1982. *Organizational Development in Health Care Organizations.* Reading, MA: Addison-Wesley.

McGregor, D. 1960. *The Human Side of Enterprise.* New York: McGraw-Hill.

Melvin, J. L. 1981. Interdisciplinary, multidisciplinary activities in ACRM. *Archives Physical and Mental Rehabilitation* 61:379–81.

Miller, D., and Friesen, P. H. 1984. *Organizations: A Quantum View.* Englewood Cliffs, NJ: Prentice-Hall.

Miller, E. C. 1978. The parallel organization structure at General Motors . . . An interview with Howard C. Carlson. *Personnel* (Sept.–Oct.): 64–69.

Miller, E. J., and Rice, A. K. 1967. *Systems of Organization.* London: Tavistock.

Mintzberg, H. 1983. *Structures in Fives.* Englewood Cliffs, NJ: Prentice-Hall.

Mohrman, A. M., Mohrman, S. A., Ledford, G. E., Cummings, T. G., and Lawler, E. E. 1989. *Large-Scale Organizational Change*. San Francisco: Jossey-Bass.

Moore, M. L. 1986. Designing parallel organizations to support organizational productivity programs. In *Handbook of Human Resources Administration*, ed. J. Famularo, pp. 4.1–4.18. New York: McGraw-Hill.

Moore, M. L., and Miners, I. A. 1988. Hidden consequences in combining OD interventions with policy and technology approaches to absence control: Implications for consultants. *Consultation* 7:86–111.

Nadler, D. A. 1977. *Feedback and Organizational Development*. Reading, MA: Addison-Wesley.

Nadler, D. A., Hanlon, M., and Lawler, E. E. 1980. Factors influencing the success of labour-management quality of work life projects. *Journal of Occupational Behaviour* 1:53–67.

Nadler, D. A., and Tushman, M. 1988. *Strategic Organizational Design*. Glenview, IL: Scott, Foresman.

Nord, W. R., and Tucker, S. 1987. *Implementing Routine and Radical Innovations*. Lexington, MA: D.C. Heath.

Oshry, B. 1988. *The Possibilities of Organization*. Boston: Power & Systems, Inc.

———. 1980. *Middle Power*. Boston: Power & Systems, Inc.

———. 1977. *Power and Position*. Boston: Power & Systems, Inc.

Pascale, R. T., and Athos, A. G. 1981. *The Art of Japanese Management*. New York: Simon & Schuster.

Pasmore, W. A. 1988. *Designing Effective Organizations: The Sociotechnical Systems Perspective*. New York: Wiley.

Pasmore, W. A., Francis, C., Haldeman, J., and Shani, A. B. 1982. Sociotechnical systems: A North American reflection on empirical studies of the seventies. *Human Relations* 35:1179–1204.

Pasmore, W. A., and Friedlander, F. 1982. An action research program for increasing employee involvement in problem solving. *Administrative Science Quarterly* 27:343–62.

Pasmore, W. A., Petee, J., and Bastian, R. 1986. Sociotechnical systems in health care: A field experiment. *Journal of Applied Behavioral Science* 22:329–39.

Pasmore, W. A., Shani, A., and Mietus, J. 1982. Technological change and work organization in the US Army: A field experiment. In *Work Organization and Technological Change,* eds. G. Mensch and R. Michans, pp. 153–56. New York: Plenum Press.

Pava, C. 1986. Redesigning sociotechnical systems design: Concepts and methods for the 1990's. *Journal of Applied Behavioral Science* 22:201–21.

Peters, M., and Robinson, V. 1984. The origins and status of action research. *Journal of Applied Behavioral Science* 20:113–24.

Polanyi, M. 1966. *The Tacit Dimension.* New York: Anchor.

Prigogine, I., and Stengers, I. 1984. *Order Out of Chaos.* Boulder, CO: New Science Library.

Reason, P., ed. 1988. *Human Inquiry in Action.* London, UK: Sage.

Rubinstein, D., and Woodman, R. W. 1984. Spiderman and the Burma raiders: Collateral organization theory in action. *Journal of Applied Behavioral Science* 20:1–21.

Saborosky, A. N., Thompson, J. C., and McPherson, K. A. 1982. Organized anarchies: Military bureaucracy in the 1980's. *Journal of Applied Behavioral Science* 18:137–53.

Schein, E. H. 1987. *The Clinical Perspective in Field Work.* Newbury Park, CA: Sage.

———. 1988. *Process Consultation, Volume 1.* Reading, MA: Addison-Wesley.

Schein, V. E., and Greiner, L. E. 1977. Can organization development be fine tuned to bureaucracies? *Organizational Dynamics* (Winter): 48–61.

Schoonhoven, C. B. 1986. Sociotechnical considerations for the development of the space station. *Journal of Applied Behavioral Science* 22:271–86.

Schultheiss, E. E. 1988. *Optimizing the Organization.* Cambridge, MA: Ballinger.

Semler, R. 1989. Managing without managers. *Harvard Business Review* (Sept.–Oct.): 76–84.

Shani, A. B., and Bushe, G. R. 1987. Visionary action research: A consultation process perspective. *Consultation* 6:3–19.

Shani, A. B., and Eberhardt, B. 1987. Parallel organization in a health care institution. *Group and Organization Studies* 12:147–73.

Shani, A. B., and Elliott, O. 1990. Sociotechnical system design in transition. In *The Emerging Practice of Organization Development*, eds. W. Sikes, A. Drexler, and J. Gant. La Jolla, CA: University Associates.

——. 1988. Applying sociotechnical systems design at the strategic apex: An illustration. *Organization Development Journal* (Summer): 53–66.

Shani, A. B., and Pasmore, W. A. 1985. Organization inquiry: Towards a new paradigm of the action research process. In *Contemporary Organization Development*, ed. D. Warrick, pp. 438–48. Glenview, IL: Scott, Foresman.

Shea, G. P. 1986. Quality circles: The danger of bottled change. *Sloan Management Review* (Spring): 3–46.

Sheldrake, R. 1981. *A New Science of Life*. Los Angeles: Tarcher.

Smith, K. K. 1982. *Groups in Conflict*. Dubuque, IA: Kendall/Hunt.

Stein, B. A., and Kanter, R. M. 1980. Building the parallel organization: Creating mechanisms for permanent quality of work life. *Journal of Applied Behavioral Science* 16:371–88.

Susman, G. I. 1981. Planned change: Prospects for the 1980's. *Management Science* 27:139–54.

Susman, G. I., and Evered, R. D. 1978. An assessment of the scientific merit of action research. *Administrative Science Quarterly* 23:583–603.

Tannenbaum, A. S., ed. 1968. *Control in Organizations*. New York: McGraw-Hill.

Taylor, D. M., and Moghaddam, F. M. 1987. *Theories of Intergroup Relations*. New York: Praeger.

Tichy, N. M. 1983. *Managing Strategic Change*. New York: Wiley

Trist, E. L. 1981. *The Evolution of Sociotechnical Systems*. Toronto, Ontario: Ontario Quality of Work Life Centre

Watzlawick, P., Weakland, J. H., and Fisch, R. 1974. *Change*. New York Norton.

Weisbord, M. R., and Stoelwinder, J. II 1979. Linking physicians, hospital management, cost containment and better patient care. *Health Care Management Review* 4.

Zand, D. E. 1974. Collateral organization: A new change strategy. *Journal of Applied Behavioral Science* 10:63–89.

——— 1981. *Information, Organization and Power.* New York: McGraw-Hill

Index